Olave Baden-Powell

Olave Baden-Powell

The authorised biography of the World Chief Guide

by

EILEEN K. WADE

HODDER AND STOUGHTON
LONDON SYDNEY AUCKLAND TORONTO

Acknowledgments

I wish to express my thanks to those who have helped me to make this story complete; especially to Lady Baden-Powell herself for her loan of diaries and letters; and to Mr William Hillcourt, Lady Bettie Walker and Mrs E. Dennis Smith who have read and checked parts of the manuscript; also to those many writers into whose books I have dipped for the purpose of establishing dates and facts.

EILEEN K. WADE

Contents

Illustrations

Key to Acknowledgments—

1   The Central Press Photos Ltd.
2   R. J. Frogley, Casino, N.S.W.
3   Persfotobureau "T STICHT", Utrecht
4   The Associated Press Ltd.
5   Keystone Press Agency Ltd.
6   United Press International (UK) Ltd.
7   The *Courier-Mail*, Brisbane
8   Weigel Studio, Christchurch, N.Z.
9   London Express News and Feature Services

Nature's Joyous Riot

The Sky, the Earth, the Sea—and all that in them is :
The far-off worlds in boundless spheres of space.
The sunshine breathing life within our Mother Earth :
The oceans with their tides and teeming depths.

The Sky, the Sea, the Earth—and all that in them is :
Linked 'neath a triune arc—of Hope and Faith and Love.
This God's Bow gleaming through the darkling forest aisles
Inspires the light for cloisters built by men.

The Earth, the Sea, the Sky—and all that in them is :
A motley, live and joyous family
All pulsing hand and hand in good accord
As comrades in the Maker's mighty scheme.

The Trefoil marks an inner band of blue—the Guides
Whose aim is laid to find, and show, the way :
To play their part in service for the whole,
And bring about great new-born fruits of Love.

R. B-P.
1924

CHAPTER I

Happy Birthday

"LET us now give the Chief Guide our loving applause," said the Dean. He was speaking from his pulpit in Westminster Abbey to over three thousand Scouts and Guides, Cubs and Brownies; and he himself led the clapping, which lasted for several minutes, before he continued his address.

It was a unique occasion; unique for the ancient Abbey and its staff; unique for the youngsters who found themselves squeezed in threes and fours into single V.I.P. seats in the chancel or sitting cross-legged on the floor just wherever they could find a vacant space; unique certainly for the World Chief Guide herself. She had travelled in most countries in the world and taken part in services in great Cathedrals as well as in small churches of many denominations, for "Duty to God" is the Guide's first Promise and this involves worship as well as service. But she had never yet read a Lesson in Westminster Abbey nor received the greetings of her family—her personal family as well as the Scouts and Guides—in such sacred and historic surroundings.

It was Thinking Day for the Guides and Founder's Day for the Scouts. February 22nd, happening to be the joint birthday of the Baden-Powells, had been chosen many years ago for this annual act of thought and remembrance.

February 22nd 1969, though, was a very special occasion, in that, as well as thinking of and praying for their fellow-members around the world, the Scouts and Guides were able to have with them, on this her eightieth birthday, that much-loved figure the widow of their Founder and the continuer of his work.

From early morning Westminster Bridge and the streets round the Abbey had been ringing with the voices and laughter of young people. It was Saturday and the normal traffic to and from the Lords and Commons, and the offices in Whitehall, had given place to numbers of buses, coaches and cars which deposited their lively cargo near the entrance to Dean's Yard. From the Underground, too, were disgorged hordes of girls and boys—with their larger escorts—clutching their lunch packets, their anoraks and other possessions, as they proceeded in orderly fashion through the purlieus of the Houses of Parliament towards the Abbey entrances. The Abbey, stretched to capacity, seemed as though it could never contain this medley of determined young people, but somehow, somewhere, seats were found and no-one was turned away. Even late-comers had the good fortune to be escorted up the central aisle to be perched on hassocks with their backs resting against the already well filled choir stalls.

Silence fell as the Dean's procession, led by the great Cross of Westminster, entered and moved with slow dignity towards the high altar. Then followed the national flag and the green, blue and gold of Scout and Guide Colours, the Commonwealth Chief Commissioner of the Guides, Mrs Parker Bowles, and the Commonwealth Chief Scout, Sir Charles Maclean. The Colour Party with the Chief Guide's personal standard followed and, last of all, walking alone and smiling to right and left, came the person on whom all eyes were focused—Olave Lady Baden-Powell, the World Chief Guide.

From the pulpit the Dean spoke of the three birthday gifts which he would like to see bestowed on her. When the greetings and applause— the first of these—had died down, he went on to suggest that she should also be given those extra Scouts and Guides, Cubs, Brownies and leaders, for which she had asked, and—last but most important of all— their renewed Promises of Duty to God and service of their fellows.

The Lesson, from I Corinthians 13, read in a clear ringing voice by the Chief Guide, was all about love, and there was a great deal of love abroad in the old Abbey that day as prayers were said, hymns sung, and Promises reaffirmed, led in turn by a Scout and a Guide.

After the wreaths had been laid at the Founder's memorial, the final prayers said, and the Blessing given by the Dean, the congregation filed past the stone and moved out into the chill February morning to greet their friends and make their various ways back to everyday life, warmed and stirred by the uplifting moment in which they had been privileged to share, and by the thought of the thousands of their fellows, scattered round the seven seas, who were with them in spirit that day.

Within the Abbey all was silence as the voices and footsteps died away.

CHAPTER II

Mother of Millions

"HER charm seems to be inexhaustible," wrote one of her American "children" of the World Chief Guide, and "charming" is perhaps the best single-word description that one could give of the octogenarian head of the largest girls' movement in the world.

"Charm" is one of those interesting words that baffle exact definition. It is something much more than mere beauty though sometimes allied with it. Charm, surely, is from within; the soul shining through the eyes, the friendly thoughts showing themselves in unselfish actions, and the radiant spirit of goodwill which produces words of real sympathy and understanding.

The first thing the stranger will notice about Olave Baden-Powell is her smile—and indeed the last thing too. Like that of the Cheshire Cat the smile seems to remain after its owner has gone; and even if you only hear her talk over the air you may be sure that the smile is there, for it is not one of politeness put on for an occasion but of honest-to-goodness enjoyment of what she is doing. And it is a most infectious smile. How often has one watched the faces of a Guide or Brownie Guard of Honour, or of the audience in a village hall, light up one after another, like the old Victorian street lamps, as she passes down the row. People feel it quite impossible not to give an answering grin when they meet the sparkling eyes and smiling mouth face to face.

Another thing which stands out about the World Chief Guide today is her apparently tireless energy, her upright figure and firm tread, and her sturdy imperviousness to weather—a subject which, like illness, seldom comes into her conversation. She is no dispenser of "inside information" to visitors and friends.

In her young days she lived an outdoor life, riding, rowing, skating, and playing every sort of energetic game. Now, when she can steal an hour or two from her typewriter, she gardens furiously, thus gaining exercise and relaxation to fit her for her most exacting task.

The Chief Guide's stately apartment in the old Thames-side Palace of Hampton Court is the home to which she returns in between those overseas journeys which occupy so much of her time. These tours, clamoured for and deeply appreciated by the girls and their leaders in many lands, take her not only to the flourishing cities and towns of the world but also to meet little struggling groups of girls in far-away mission stations strung along the African desert, to the far Northern territories of Australia, the wilds of New Guinea, and the many newly-developing industrial areas of Canada and elsewhere. It is in these smaller weaker groups, so firmly imbued with the determination to be Guides in spite of—or perhaps because of—every sort of difficulty, that their Chief sees the surest proof of the pudding for which her famous husband gave the recipe more than sixty years ago, when he suggested Guiding for the girls who wanted to be Scouts like their brothers.

Indeed large numbers of girls had already taken matters into their own hands and become "Scouts", to the great agitation of their parents, the considerable annoyance of the male members of their families, and the disapproval of the Chief Scout. While sympathising with the girls in their desire for something more lively than embroidery and piano playing, he was sure that their presence among the boys would harm the newly-formed Scout Movement. "No feminine units are to be present," was his decision when about to inspect a Boy Scout Rally.

But the girls stuck to their scouting and as early as 1909 the young Amazons were commended by a Kent newspaper:

The most striking feature was undoubtedly an interesting ambulance display by a newly-formed troop of Girl Scouts. These young ladies were in full scouting equipment and they looked charming in their neat fitting costume of blouse and short skirt of serviceable navy blue serge. Around the neck was worn a light blue silk scarf which can be used as a bandage if necessary, and they also wore the usual slouch hat. They carried poles similar to those of the Boy Scouts and on their backs were slung knapsacks containing the necessary ambulance materials . . . They showed methods of aiding a fainting person, setting broken arms, and concluded by carrying some of their numbers off the platform on stretchers formed with scouting poles and sheets taken from the knapsacks.

In the autumn of that year the girls forced themselves upon B-P's notice by appearing in Scout uniform at a big Boy Scout Rally at the Crystal Palace. Rather than disappoint them the Chief Scout duly inspected them and the "recognition" thus triumphantly gained inspired the girls to further effort. It was the insistence of these intrepid young women that really started the Girl Guides and without their enthusiasm there would have been no Guide Movement today. Though B-P is everywhere acclaimed as their Founder, he always insisted that Guiding started itself.

If, in lesser ways, time has changed fashions and methods, there are things about Baden-Powell's Movement, whether for boys or girls, that are timeless and changeless—and they are the real things. The Promise and the Law; the Good Turn; the love of camping and the open air; and the spirit of adventure and of service which attracted those first girls to join, albeit "illegally", will continue to inspire future generations. On the whole young people remain much the same, basically, as they have always been.

Meantime, in 1909, the Chief Scout began to feel that he could not let the matter rest there. To forbid something to a child was merely to encourage rebellion, so something must be done for these determined young women. After all, if his aim was character training, the acknowledged fundamental reason for Scouting, there was not much point in leaving "the other half" of the nation untrained.

So he must think again. To pour cold water on enthusiasm of any kind was against his principles.

A bachelor and a serving soldier, renowned as the Defender of Mafeking in the late war, and beginning to be known as the Founder of the Boy Scouts, B-P was not as yet recognised as one of the world's leading educationists.

He enlisted the co-operation of his sister Agnes, as the person most likely to sympathise with his ideas, and in a letter to his aunt, Lady Smyth, at the end of 1909, he was able to write:

Az and I have sketched out the enclosed suggestion for utilising the girls who want to become Boy Scouts in a more useful role. We

B

are only offering it as a suggestion and don't intend to organise it. Several hundreds of girls who were Boy Scouts (on their own appointment!) are now Girl Guides.

Several hundreds! And today there are many millions of active Girl Guides and Girl Scouts (the U.S.A. have retained the latter name), only about a fifth of whom are British. This does not include the numberless millions who have passed through the training. It is rare now to meet a man or woman who has not at some time or other been caught up in this world-wide Movement or been touched by its influence.

"I was a Guide at school," says the Air Hostess as she hands Lady Baden-Powell into her seat. "My boy is just off to his Scout camp," chimes in a fellow-passenger. "May I ask your Ladyship for an autograph for my Brownie daughter?" says the steward; and as the Press, the photographers, the radio and television staffs of the world approach the Chief Guide for interviews it is certain that among them will be members of her "family" ready with the left handshake. Mutual recognition of this kind has oiled the wheels on many occasions which might otherwise have been exacting on one side or frustrating on the other.

The left handshake, common to Scouts and Guides everywhere, and peculiar to them, has a romantic reason underlying it.

The Founder, in explaining it, used to tell the story of two tribes in Africa that were constantly at war with one another, until suddenly one day the leader of one of them had a change of heart. He came to the border of his own territory and, when the chief of the opposing tribe appeared, flung down his shield and held out his left hand in friendship, saying that here was the proof that he had come unarmed and in a new spirit. The other chief responded at once and this giving of the left hand came to be regarded as a sign of love and trust for those who live by a common Law and Promise. Hence the expression "a disarming smile".

"The Law and Promise played an enormous part in our lives," writes a Guide of the very early days. "A Guide's Honour was a treasured possession and so was the badge which we always wore to remind us of it."

In essentials the recipe given by B-P will never vary if it is to continue to capture the imagination of the young of each succeeding age. The willing spirit of Duty to God and loyalty to the country, of open-air adventure and world-wide friendship, will still appeal and the Promise and Law which bind its members will not change. But Guiding has always kept abreast of the times, as was its Founder's intention, and in its details of training, activities, and uniform, it can be adapted to the needs of each generation as well as to the traditions and skills of the various countries which have adopted it.

Olave Baden-Powell is something far more than the widow of the Founder. She has established for herself a position in Guiding which is unique. Patrons, Presidents, Chairmen, and Committee members, the Girl Guides share with other organisations—their duties are laid down; but no other organisation ever had a Chief Guide and the post is one which Olave has literally carved out for herself. Having built up the Movement from its early days she no longer takes much part in its detailed administration. She knows that it stands firmly on the foundations laid in her husband's lifetime when the early "builders" were in close touch with his ideas and determined to promote these and to hand them down to succeeding generations. She has no fears for the future for she knows that it would be difficult to destroy something that has not only survived the persecution and set-backs of two world wars —and other lesser conflicts—but has actually grown stronger thereby and come up smiling afterwards.

"What it has meant for youth and for the world", writes an elderly woman, "cannot be foretold; but what a leavening it has been in these days of indiscipline and cheap entertainment. We who have been privileged to work alongside you, however humbly, know, and it is comforting and helpful. My meetings with you have given me renewed courage, steadfastness and joy, even in the most troubled days. And I know there are, and were, many thousands who have found the same help, and it will go on wherever the B-P spirit has touched with its profound wisdom."

Olave Baden-Powell's own work today lies mainly in keeping in touch with those who look to her as their Chief and more especially with the younger leaders on whom will fall the task of handing on to their successors the spirit and ideals of the Founder.

Naturally the young folk—boys as well as girls—claim her as their own and much of her time is devoted to attending Rallies of these; but she realises that her most valuable contribution—and one which she alone can make—is her talks to their leaders, and potential leaders, whether at large gatherings or in the quiet of her own home. None who meet her ever fail to be stirred, spurred and encouraged to further effort by her unbounded enthusiasm and sympathetic appreciation of their work.

"You came so near to them," wrote a leader, "and nearer still to their hearts. You made their Guiding mean more to them than it has ever meant before; something bigger and something to reach up to and so full of happiness and friendliness. Hearts are too full to be able to express the admiration and gratitude that go out to you but you must know how much you mean to us."

There is hardly a country that the Chief Guide has not visited in order to maintain this personal touch. She has made more than six hundred and fifty flights and there are few airports where, even if the plane touched down at night, there will not be contingents of Guides— and often Scouts too—waiting to welcome her and to take her into their hearts and homes.

The leaders of many of these countries, recognising what Guiding has done not only for their own nations but in promoting world friendship, have bestowed on the World Chief Guide their high honours.

She holds, among others, the Grand Cross of the British Empire (G.B.E.), the Order of the White Rose of Finland, the Order of Merit of Poland, the Grand Cross of the Order of the Phoenix of Greece, the Merit of Honour of Haiti Republic, the Order of the Sun of Peru, the Order of Bernard O'Higgins of Chile, the Order of Vasco Nunez de Balboa, Panama, L'Ordre Nationale du Cedre de Lebanon, the Order of the Sacred Treasure of Japan, and L'Ordre Grand Ducal de la Couronne de Chene de Luxembourg. Why she has not yet received the Nobel Peace Prize remains a puzzle to those who have seen her great work for peace and goodwill.

Hundreds, and probably thousands, of women, alive today or "gone home", have made their immense contribution to the success of the

Guide Movement. They cannot all be mentioned here but they must never be forgotten. But there is no-one doing active work for the Movement today who would not agree that it is to Olave Lady Baden-Powell, widow of its great Founder, that the whole of Guiding looks for the inspiration which drives it along its happy and progressive road. She would not herself take any credit for this; she would give it all to her husband, to the programme which he invented, and to her fellow workers, past and present, who put it into operation. "There are many Movements, and all honour to them," she will say, "for doing good to young people. But ours is different. Scouts and Guides are not 'done good to'—they are expected to do good to themselves and also to help other people. The whole thing about Scouting and Guiding is that it is not a case of being disciplined by someone else but of disciplining and toughening your*self*. That is where the difference lies."

Radio, television, and tape-recording, as well as flying, have brought to the Chief Guide many fresh opportunities for carrying out her immense task, and she seizes on every new device with enthusiasm. The growth in number of World Camps and Jamborees brings her in touch—sometimes by helicopter these days—with an ever-increasing number of her family—Scouts as well as Guides.

"For I think you are the mother of all Scouts," writes an African boy from Zomba. "What a joy it must have been for you to have all your boys with you at the big Jamboree. I enjoyed it very much and I think you did for I saw you several times and you looked very happy. I was with the Malawi contingent and I thank you for the Jamboree which I will never forget."

They do not forget. Even if they experience it for only a brief year or two of their lives, something of the B-P spirit of world friendship and goodwill seems to rub off on each one, and they regard the Chief Guide as the strongest possible living link with their Founder.

A tall New Zealander, on his way to get a glimpse of the Baden-Powells' former home, Pax Hill, remarked that he had once seen B-P at a Scout Rally in Auckland. "He didn't say very much to us," he said, in fact I only remember that he began by saying 'Hallo you Blighters', but it was the way he looked at us as if he loved and trusted us. We all felt it and we knew that we must stick to Scouting."

The same thing was felt by a Scouter who had been to the Jamboree
at Arrowe Park in 1929:

I never knew B-P personally but his son Peter was in my particular
section of Sub-camp 6. The Chief Guide used to come and talk with
us and on one great day the Chief Scout reined in his big black horse
at our ropes and chatted with Peter. I made some trivial remark and
the Chief turned his head and looked at me. It may seem strange to
those who knew his every changing expression but the memory of
that one glance has stayed with me, vivid and unforgettable, ever
since . . . and I know that glance has helped me, ever since, both to
do and to avoid.

If chance encounters of that sort could have had such effect, what
must have been, on his wife, the impact of nearly thirty years of close
companionship with one of the world's greatest educators? With his
chosen material to work on, the result could hardly be other than
interesting.

One of the world's greatest educators? One makes the claim advisedly
and with a close study of what people in a position to know have written
about Baden-Powell.

Dean Russell, Professor of Education at Columbia University in the
early days of the century, said this of Scouting, whether for boys or
girls:

Our schools are long on their ability to give information—knowledge which shall be of worth to future citizens; they are competent
to go a long way in the matter of stirring the right feelings and
developing the right appreciations on the part of the citizen; but they
are all too short when it comes to fixing those habits and developing
and encouraging activities without which the individual may be a
pretty poor and even a very dangerous citizen.

It is right at this point that the scouting program supplements the
work of the schools . . . its curriculum is adjusted in such a way that the
more you study it, and the further you go into it, you who are school-
masters, the more you must be convinced that there was a discovery
made when it was put forth. . . . My friends, as a schoolmaster I want
to tell you that it is my honest conviction that our schools in America,
supported by the public for the public good, will not be equal to the

task of the next generation unless we incorporate into them as much as is possible of the Scouting spirit and the Scouting method ... When teachers sound the depths of their own patriotism and realise that upon them, more perhaps than on any other class of Americans, depends the future welfare of this country, they will not leave untested and untried an instrument that makes for so much good.

And Professor Malherbe, in South Africa, writing in *The Forum* at the time of B-P's death, said, inter alia:

Most of the tributes paid to Baden-Powell have dwelt on his achievements as a soldier. While these may be great, yet it is strange that very few people seem to realise that in Baden-Powell we had one of the greatest educators of all time and one whose name will live in the history of education long after people have forgotten him as a military man. I have often said to advanced students who come to consult me about a subject for a Ph.D. thesis—"Why don't you write a thesis on the psychological basis of the Boy Scout movement? It involves the psychology of the adolescent—the most difficult time in a young person's life—and is a study with fascinating possibilities."

One last quotation: in *Challenge to Heritage* Ruth Anderson Oakley wrote:

Lord Baden-Powell has been one of the greatest friends of the child for, with the genius of understanding the noble depths of his nature, he gave in the Scout and Guide Movement the essential elements to arouse them. The foundations of character and intelligence are laid by capturing the spirit of happiness, emotion and energy into activity, fieldcraft, skill, physical health, service and fellowship. These are the wealth of humanity and only when we are given a chance to develop them shall we have contented men.

Those are just three out of very many testimonies to Baden-Powell as an educator. His was the genius, the moving spirit, the skill, that fabricated the tool which he put into the hands of his followers and which, by his own personality, he used for the benefit of so many.

How does his widow, the World Chief Guide, use the tool bequeathed to her?

It must be a happiness for a "Mother of Millions" to hear sometimes just what her family feels in the depths of its heart . . . I now venture to tell you how one member feels. The debt of gratitude that I owe to Guiding is so tremendous that it is not possible to think in terms of repayment. As a youngster the finding of ideals that one was searching for and longing to follow. As a young woman the joys of camping and discovering the secrets of nature out of doors; as a grown woman the joys of trainings and conferences where one met so many lovely people. In recent years travels abroad, contacts made in an even wider circle; work with the Extensions and the lessons learned from their pain bravely borne, handicapped lives usefully lived, poverty borne with patience and without complaint. All this I have received from Guiding and without it my life would have been impoverished . . . What can I do to repay just a tiny bit of such an enormous debt? You showed me in two words spoken from the platform—by Goodness and Kindness.

CHAPTER III

The Child

"Every childhood is a meadow. There may be weeds and stony places in it, but there is sweet grass too in patches, and days of sun and freedom and happiness . . . and at its end there is the gate to the outside, and it opens for each one of us—opens only once."

IT would be illuminating, when writing a biography, to be able to begin at the very beginning and to show the many influences and characteristics, handed down through generations, which had their part in shaping the subject of a story. But in such case the book would become unwieldy even before the main point was arrived at. So let us find someone within reasonable distance from whom to make a beginning.

We do not know a great deal about Archdeacon Wilkins of Nottingham—a thoroughly respectable-sounding ancestor—in Jane Austen's understanding of the word, i.e. worthy of respect. He was born on May 22nd 1785 and married in 1811 Amelia Auriol Hay Drummond, by whom he had fifteen children, quite a tidy family even for those days. Nine sons and six daughters to feed, clothe and educate! One only hopes he had a good stipend.

What is important for this book, however, is that the Wilkinses did not decide that ten children were enough, for it was their eleventh child and fifth daughter, born in 1827, who married George Hill. The Hills' daughter, Katharine, married Harold Soames in 1883, and in 1889 Olave St Clair, their third and youngest child, was born on February 22nd, a date now familiar to very many people throughout the world as the "Thinking Day" of the Guides.

The George Hills were not very well off, having had severe money losses as well as a large family, and their girls had not only to turn their hands to many domestic chores but also for a time to go out and earn their keep as companions or governesses—almost the only openings in those days for girls of their upbringing.

So it must have been something of a relief to her parents, as well as a great joy to Katharine, a beautiful girl, when Harold Soames met her at the house of her employers, fell in love with her and carried her off to a home of her own. He was not at that time a wealthy man but his father, a successful maltster, had given him a brewery business to work up, and it must have been everything to him to find a wife who was not only lovely to look at but also domestically expert and able to manage a home and children with very little outside help. Their staff at first consisted of one old woman to help in the house and an aged handy-man gardener.

Harold Soames had no love for business but he set to work with a will to put the brewery on a firm footing as quickly as possible in order the sooner to be able to leave it in other hands. The brewery was situated in Chesterfield, and it was at Stubbing Court, five miles south-west of that town, that his three children were born. Stubbing Court was a solid Georgian house, standing in a park and surrounded by woods—rather an isolated home for the young wife with her three babies. Five miles to and from work for her husband, before the days of the motor car, must have involved some effort, but he managed it, riding or walking the distance every day until Olave, their youngest child, was a year old. Then it was decided to move to a house in the town, set among fields but within easy reach of the office.

Chesterfield was once a Roman station on the road from Derby to York. In more modern times its chief claim to fame has been the unusual twisted spire on its parish church—probably due to the action of the sun upon the lead, warping timbers that had not been thoroughly seasoned.

At West House the young mother felt less cut off from the world and it was a pleasant home for the three children who loved to watch the horse fairs which took place in the fields opposite the nursery windows —fields which later became the terminus of the railway which was in process of being built.

Sunday was a day of rest for horses as well as for people, and the children loved to visit the fine brewery horses taking their weekly respite in the stables—and to be lifted up to stroke their satiny faces.

West House was an attractive red brick building with panelled rooms and Adam chimney pieces. Behind its high garden walls the Soameses lived a quiet serene life, and tiny Olave, with her big brown eyes and ready smile, was the admiration and plaything of visitors as well as a joy to her parents. By 1893 the time had come for the two elder children to have a nursery governess, and Miss Wilson, who had been a junior mistress at the local Grammar School, joined the household and remained for four years. Though too small to join in the lessons of Auriol and Arthur, Olave shared in their walks with "Wissie" and much enjoyed the stories that she was always ready to tell.

In 1895 the family moved again. Harold Soames was not a man who could ever settle down anywhere. He was a nervous dyspeptic, a seeker after beauty in nature and art, a connoisseur of architecture, and an artist of some ability. No sooner had the little family established itself in a home of his choice than he was impatient to be off again in search of something different. In many ways he must have been a very difficult man to live with but he was devoted to them all and adored his youngest child though she had at first disappointed him by not being the Olaf of his hopes. Hence her first name of Olave.

A Derbyshire neighbour, Sir George Sitwell, had a mind which ran on much the same lines as that of Harold Soames and though he owned the beautiful Renishaw Hall, famed for its gardens, furniture, pictures and tapestries, he was willing to let it to Mr Soames for some months and to remove himself and his family further afield. He also had a house at Scarborough, which place he represented in Parliament.

During the Commonwealth struggles Sir George's forebear, Mr George Sitwell of Renishaw, had suffered severely for his loyalty and after the Restoration had retrieved his fortune by establishing iron works which did a large trade. Before his death in 1667 he had placed in his house the exquisite tapestries of Judoc de Vos of Brussels, which became a great feature of the place.

The Soames children were not of an age to appreciate such things and Olave's early memories are of fun and games in the park and of three cart horses who unexpectedly strolled into the front hall one fine day. There was a lake in the grounds and the children had their earliest lessons in boat-handling.

Now Arthur was sent away to school at Bilton Grange, near Rugby, and lessons were due to begin for the little girls with a German governess "Frieda" who replaced their loved Wissie and who, like the former, remained a life-long friend of Olave. The governess's first impression of her younger pupil was of a small untidy child, dressed in Wellington boots and with a scarlet tam-o-shanter on her tousled dark hair, with a collie and a huge St Bernard in tow.

Olave was learning to knit and had made, with great effort, a "comforter" for one of the keepers on the estate. Her hair had been cut short like a boy's. Proud of her handiwork she carried it out and formally presented it to the old gentleman. "And what did he say?" enquired her mother.

"He said 'Thank you my little man,'" replied Olave.

"And what did you say to that?"

"Well," said Olave grandly, "I didn't undeceive him as I thought it might hurt his feelings."

In her love of adventure and exploration the child nearly lost her life at Renishaw by falling over the banisters onto a glass roof, and would undoubtedly have killed herself but for the presence of mind of Auriol who screamed and clung to the edge of her clothing until help came. But her little head was rather severely injured and just at the time when their lease had come to an end and Sir George, with his house party, was due to return. The Sitwells were kindness itself, kept the little invalid until she was fit to be moved, and visited her with grapes and other suitable delicacies at the hands of Osbert.

After this experience serious lessons for Olave were in abeyance, and the child was ordered by the doctor to lead an open-air life—which was much more to her taste.

The next move was to Bryerswood, a charming house with a fine view overlooking the lake at Windermere. Here lessons out of doors became the fashion, and little Olave learned by easy stages to read and write while developing her love of the natural world around her. Books were carried out onto the moor and Mrs Soames would bring out a picnic lunch for them all. The two little girls with their governess spent happy days filling their lungs with the pure lakeland air and learning with Frieda to sing the old folk songs and rounds as they walked over the moor.

Restless as ever, Harold Soames was now tired of the bleak northern climate and took a house in London at 18 St James's Place. He had handed over his irksome business to a company and was a free man, able to live on his dividends. Leaving the family in London he went off to Italy to paint.

London life did not suit the child Olave and she had one illness after another. She was still delicate and pined for the fresh freedom of the outdoor world. So once more it was time to move and a country home was found in 1898 at Pixton Park, near Dulverton in Somerset. This was Olave's sixth home in nine short years. Its owner, the Earl of Carnarvon, had two other houses so was pleased to let Pixton for a time.

To Katharine this constant uprooting by her husband must have been a tiresome business but to the children it was fun and to Olave a grand adventure. She loved home-making then, as she does today, and to unpack the family treasures and settle their pets into new quarters was always exciting. Her mother gave her the character of being "equal to three charwomen in work, and to the whole race in wits, as she hurls her sweet energy and thought into every corner, and masters at once the intricacies of staircase and passage from dungeon to garret."

At Pixton, with its spacious grounds and heronry, there opened to the children many fresh delights in the keeping of doves, chickens, and other pets. Anything in fur or feathers would do for Olave to love and serve and each hen had its name and a personality understood by its owner. Pixton was in many ways an ideal spot, with plenty of room for all their hobbies and pursuits; but it was not to be for long, another move was in the air.

The Marquis of Salisbury was even better housed than Lord Carnarvon. Arlington Street in London, Hatfield in Hertfordshire, Childwall Hall in Liverpool, and Cranborne Manor near Salisbury, gave him a fine choice of residences, and he was willing to let Cranborne to Mr Soames in the spring of 1899. So, after a winter in hotels in Bournemouth, where the children had dancing classes and gymnastics, with elocution lessons for Olave, the family arrived at Cranborne Manor—perhaps the most beautiful of all Olave's childhood homes. Dating from the time of Athelstane, it had been a hunting box of King John when pursuing the deer on Cranborne Chase. Later the Chase changed hands several times but from Edward IV to James I it was again the property of the Crown. It was then granted to William Cecil, Earl of Salisbury.

By 1830 there were some twelve thousand deer within a circle of thirty miles but the hunting of these animals was deteriorating from "sport" to "deer-stealing"—and the keepers and even the hunters themselves sometimes met their death there as well as the deer. Towards the close of the nineteenth century what had once been "the sport of kings" had become "a nursery for and temptation to all kinds of vice, profligacy and immorality". Smugglers, outlaws, and vagabonds of all kinds resorted there and in 1840 the Chase was disafforested.

In these historic surroundings, among the smooth green lawns of Cranborne Manor—mown for hundreds of years—bowling alley and tennis courts, Olave began to take an interest in outdoor games. Her father, who was a very good tennis player, taught her to play the game and she also began to ride. At Cranborne, as well as turning their poultry keeping into a real "business" concern and selling eggs to the house, the children could have ponies and dogs and other pets to tend and adore. Life was fine and from Olave's point of view left little to be desired. When no live animals were available Tweety and Piggles, her inanimate mascots, were about her bed and shared her adventures.

Lessons, of course, had to be endured, and arithmetic "which I positively hate" came on Olave's time-table twice in every week. But it was more pleasurable when it took the form of adding up her poultry accounts and banking her profits.

The Soameses were introverts, with few interests outside their home. They loved their three children in a somewhat possessive fashion. Arthur, "Boogie", was the special hero and darling of his mother, Auriol the decorative one whom it was the greatest fun to dress, and little Olave the practical and sensible helper, always at hand to carry messages, to see to everybody's comfort and make herself useful. She was friends with everyone, whether in the drawing-room or the servants' hall, was nearly always laughing, and never walked if she could skip or run.

For all children, "home" is where their parents are, and, in spite of the many moves, these children had security and a happy background in their formative years. Arthur was destined for Eton and the Guards, and the girls—well, surely they would marry "suitably" when the time came. Such was the philosophy of most well-to-do parents in those far-off days when, under the peaceful reign of Queen Victoria, England was building her Empire, secure in her right little tight little island home.

And yet one wonders at how little even the best parents know of their children's needs. In the book which Katharine Soames wrote by hand, a copy for each of her three children, there occur long passages expressing her desire for Olave's future happiness, that she shall always "live her best and give her best"—and yet, at a crisis in her daughter's life, when she was handing herself over to her life's work, that same mother was to do everything in her power to frustrate it, to turn her thoughts from it, to beg her to give it all up. When carrying out her Guide work Olave might never mention to her mother the subject nearest to her heart, nor be seen by her in uniform. It was a heavy sentence.

That time was still undreamed of when the little girl accompanied her parents to the Riviera for her first trip abroad. Temporarily bereft of her home pets she made firm friends with the sturdy little donkeys who were their means of transport up the mountain paths.

A large part of Mentone was very quaint and old, all built up a hill, with steep stone stairways as the only roads for getting to the houses. No carts could get there so all the food and things needed had to be carried by hand, in sacks and baskets, or on peoples' shoulders or even on their heads.

But when the things were furniture or large packing cases, these would be dumped on the backs of donkeys and it would be quite an ordinary thing to see a tiny donkey walking up a steep flight of stone stairs carrying a bed or a wardrobe on its back.

Besides this hard work for them there were also plenty of donkeys to be used for pleasure. It was lovely to go off for long day expeditions riding these dear little creatures up the mountains to visit the mediaeval looking villages perched like nests on the lovely hills inland.

A lover of music, Olave now began to learn to play the violin and to take a real interest in her lessons, encouraged by a great friend, Sybil Mounsey-Heysham, who, in Olave's eyes, did everything perfectly, whether playing the violin, riding, sailing, bird-watching or stalking the wild life. Many of the exciting activities of the Guides and Scouts of today were practised by these two girls who both revelled in anything connected with the outdoor world.

When he saw that Olave was going to stick to her violin playing, her father gave her a fine instrument, a copy of a Stradivarius, made by Messrs Hill for the Paris Exhibition. In London, where they went for the winter months, she studied later for a time under Herr Graaf and joined an orchestra. Auriol was a good pianist and the three girls enjoyed playing trios together.

Olave kept up her fiddling for a little time after her marriage but the more onerous duties of Chief Guide left little time for practice, and Sybil Mounsey-Heysham took over the violin and handed it to the Girl Guides Association for use, on loan, by promising Guide violinists.

Olave has always been grateful for this time of studying and playing an instrument, which gave her an insight into the best music and a real appreciation of what it can bring to life.

By the time she was twelve and a half—when many girls of her age were going to their first boarding schools—Olave's education was pronounced by her parents to be complete, as regarded governesses and book-learning.

Arthur was away at school, Auriol was fast growing into a young lady, and the fond parents, after looking over a recommended school in Surrey, decided to keep their youngest child at home, whether entirely for her benefit or their own seems doubtful. As it happened, however, the education gained haphazardly, through the constant companionship of cultured parents and their friends, was singularly happily chosen for fitting Olave for the life that was to be hers.

A criticism that one has heard of education today is that too much passes from the note-book of the teacher to the note-book of the student without ever passing through the mind of either! A cynical exaggeration, no doubt, but it has certainly not always been recognised that true education consists in the drawing out of what is there rather than in the pushing in of facts.

Olave never went to school even for a day, never sat for any sort of examination or passed any test, and yet no-one could say that she was not an educated person. Gaps there were of course, and she has been the first to recognise this and to take an opposite course with her own

Age six, with her hair cut
short like a boy's

With her dogs at Renishaw

Age twenty

Her first meeting with B-P on the
Arcadian, January, 1912

At Grey Rigg, 1912

In her first Guide uniform
as Chief Commissioner, 1916

children later on. The ability to speak fluently two or three languages might have been a great asset, but she can do more with halting French, with handshakes, gestures and smiles, than many people could do with the correctly spoken word.

At the time, to a child who cordially disliked school books and school rooms, the arrangement seemed ideal. The cloistered life came to an abrupt end, and she was free. "Having given up all book work," she wrote in the diary which she began at the age of eleven and has continued ever since, "I have more leisure for Tompy, for Doogy, and the rest of my pets."

An uninterrupted régime of outdoor life, tennis, bicycling, riding and driving, brought colour to her cheeks and vigour to her limbs and she was no longer the delicate child of the family.

At Purley Hall, their next home near Pangbourne in Berkshire, she learned on the river to swim and to row, two useful and health-giving activities which in those days might conceivably have been omitted from any school curriculum. When they were not spending whole days in and on the river there was a small farm to be enjoyed and the children revelled in the hay-making. Olave's rough little horse, Tompy, became one of her greatest friends and allies and no human being could have been more devotedly served in sickness and in health.

In 1903 Olave paid her first visit to Scotland, a country which she has loved ever since that first bicycle tour of nearly seventy years ago.

Bicycling was a new craze at the turn of the century, and in the comparatively trafficless roads there was nothing to prevent young people from exploring the countryside in this leisurely fashion. Their method of travel to Scotland would seem to the businessman of today an odd way of reaching the grouse moor which was Harold Soames's objective. Sending the servants on ahead, to prepare the house which had been rented for two months, the family travelled by train to Carlisle. There the two horses were put into the shafts and were driven in easy stages by Mrs Soames through Kirkcudbrightshire, the groom sitting up behind and the children on their bicycles following the same route.

Here among the grouse and heather happy days were spent driving and bicycling and picnicing, visiting and entertaining friends, until autumn brought them south once more.

C

From Purley to beautiful Luscombe Castle, Dawlish, was Harold Soames's next move, and here Olave was able to perfect her swimming and water pursuits in her first real seaside home. She also practised on her violin for hours each day, and was confirmed by the Bishop of Crediton in Dawlish church. This latter event she took seriously, recognising her future responsibility as a Christian "on her own". It must have been at this time that she first began to wonder what life was for and whether anything more than day to day enjoyment was required of her by her Maker.

A year later the family moved to Bradfield, near Cullompton, a beautiful Tudor house complete with a banqueting hall forty-four feet long, and a minstrels' gallery. Here, in her first "grown-up" home, Olave unwillingly let down her skirts, put up her hair, and "came out" at a ball given for her by her parents. She was rather shy, did not enjoy social occasions, and would really have preferred to be in the stable with her horse. Though she had plenty of partners and many admirers, dancing was not one of her favourite occupations and she cordially disliked the rather meaningless social life of the débutante, still finding her greatest fun in the out of doors and in her childish ploys.

The owner of Bradfield, Lord Waleran, paid a visit to his property one day and was surprised to find Olave with a young friend "boating" in the lake in the saucer baths more usually to be found in the bedrooms of the period. He laughed and said, "I never knew what baths were for before."

From the West Country the Soameses now moved to Suffolk, where Harold had found an historic house—Hardwick—near Bury St Edmund's. Built by Robert Drury in the reign of Henry VIII and rebuilt in 1681, the house was full of antique marbles and treasured relics of Napoleon, Horace Walpole, and others renowned in history. Olave's comment, however, was that "there is nothing specially nice indoors, very dark and rambling and all steps. But the Italian formal garden is lovely and there is a fountain in the middle of it in a stone basin in which Auriol and I intend to bathe."

They arrived at Hardwick in May 1907 and spent the first few months in a ceaseless round of tennis with the young people of the neighbourhood. There was an indoor tennis court in the riding school so weather made little difference to their enjoyment. All play and no work can pall and Olave now confessed to being bored "for the first time in my life almost. Horrid child I am to be bored when I have everything I could wish for except, perhaps, a hunter."

This wish was soon to be fulfilled. On June 13th "Harper, the horse-dealer, brought a big cob for us to try. I rode and drove him with Zephyr and he was so nice and good that we bought him at once for £40."

Pedro, as they named him, was all very well for ordinary riding and driving, but on hunting days Olave was more usually mounted on a horse lent to her by the agent, a dangerous animal on which she cheerfully risked her neck.

Mrs Soames had grown tired of being what she called "Suffolk-ated" and withdrew with Auriol to their flat in London, leaving Olave and her father together to do the things that they both enjoyed.

When it was too hard for hunting—and it was an exceptionally hard winter—Olave added skating to her accomplishments and grew to love the rhythmic motion so much that she continued to skate at Prince's when they went back to London.

Now, at long last, Harold Soames contemplated settling down, and decided to buy a house and live in it. Grey Rigg, Lilliput, near Parkstone in Dorset, was to be their permanent home and it was a joy to Olave and her mother to feel that they could have all their own things about them at last—and make a garden.

The name of Lilliput in *Gulliver's Travels* is owed to the fact that Dean Swift lived in the village while writing the book.

At Grey Rigg Olave lived what she describes as a life of idle pleasure, though one cannot imagine her ever having an unoccupied moment. It was a life which, though outwardly happy, her now sensitive conscience could not approve. She felt herself to be in a trap and unable to escape. Auriol was busy being social in London and managing her many suitors, so Olave was the "home" daughter, indispensable—so they thought—to her parents and unable to take herself away to do a job. Even her small effort at amusing and teaching small boys in a Bournemouth home, run by the Invalid Children's Aid Association, was frowned upon when it took her away for a day from the tennis or squash court, and this work was subjected to constant interruptions. Her "ineffable longings" to do something useful and worthwhile in the world were thwarted and, short of marriage, there seemed to be no escape from the life she was leading.

Nor was the social round of London, where they went for weeks at a time, any more in her line though it was just bearable when she was able to have her beloved dog with her.

In London that wonderful ballerina, Anna Pavlova, was dancing her famous "Dying Swan"—prophetic indeed, for the London that so many knew in those last days before the 1914 war, and which so few remember now, was assuredly having its swan-song. Never again would be seen such contrasts, such opulence on the one hand and such poverty on the other. There was no Welfare State, no pension scheme for the old, and the wealthy wearers of evening dress who climbed red-carpeted stairs each evening in the fashionable London squares, on their way to a ball, a "salon" or a musical party, looked down on pathetic beggars hoping for a few coppers to fall from the golden purses. While kid-booted white-frocked children walked with their nannies in the park, the "other" children went to school wearing father's cast-off coats, wrinkled tattered stockings and broken boots. Large staffs of indoor servants, waiting on perhaps one or two people, lived like trolls in basement rooms, emerging up the area steps to see the light of day once or twice a week.

Thoughtful people—and Olave was one—felt that there must be something wrong somewhere, and she longed to do something to help. One quarter of her life had gone—and to what purpose?

Yet, for the "haves" it was pleasant to be part of "the season", to dance at the Ritz and sup off plovers' eggs at the Savoy after the play; to frequent the Opera and to see the great actors of the day in their theatres—Irving, Tree, Forbes Robertson, Mary Anderson, Gerald du Maurier and the rest; to attend concerts where the best performers were to be heard; to skate at Prince's and watch polo at Ranelagh, Hurlingham or Roehampton.

If Olave had inherited some of her father's restless energy, with her it was not that she wanted change for its own sake, but that she had a feeling of guilt at having so much, when others had so little, to make life enjoyable.

She wrote privately to a London hospital to enquire about the possibility of taking up a nursing career, but the reply was discouraging

—she was too young. She longed to do something useful but now she could only mark time and count the blessings that were hers.

Meantime life at Grey Rigg was pleasanter than London. Motoring had become a general craze in 1909 and Harold Soames bought one of the new cars and engaged a chauffeur. Motor excursions, tennis tournaments, picnics, bathing, sailing and riding were the order of every day and though Olave confided to her diary "another year gone by and wasted" she was outwardly enjoying it all and taking it in her stride. There were several eligible young men and she could have married—but she was waiting for something, she knew not what.

CHAPTER IV

Arcadian Days

LIFE is unpredictable, and therein lies most of its fascination. A letter by the morning post may seal your fate; or you may open your front door turn left instead of right as you had intended, and the whole course of your life may be changed.

This book is an attempt to show how the World Chief Guide, Olave Lady Baden-Powell, G.B.E., a name to conjure with in almost any corner of the world, came to achieve this position.

We might perhaps have called this chapter "A Tale of Two Tickets".

Harold Soames could well afford to take a cruise to sunshine when winter came, and it had become his custom to take a daughter with him. In 1909 Olave had accompanied him on a cruise to Norway, where she delighted in the lovely scenery and the friendly courteous people whom, in later years, she has grown to know so intimately.

In 1910 it had been Auriol's turn and she had been with her father to India and had in 1911 become engaged and married to a man whom she had met on board ship, Robert Davidson. So now Olave was again to be her father's companion, and at Auriol's wedding reception, where she was her sister's chief bridesmaid, they met a friend who persuaded Mr Soames to apply for a couple of berths in the *Arcadian* about to make her maiden voyage in a winter trip to the West Indies.

Reluctant though she was to leave her dogs and horses even for a few weeks, Olave naturally looked forward to life on board ship. Who wouldn't, that was heart-whole, attractive, and twenty-three?

They wrote for passages but their application was turned down—too late, the passenger list was complete, and Harold Soames turned his mind to other schemes. Then, at the very last minute, came a letter to say that two passages had been cancelled through unforeseen circumstances. They could have the places.

It was a foggy winter morning when father and daughter drove to

Southampton. There was a dock strike and the passengers stood about waiting for a tug to take them out to the *Arcadian*, lying anchored in deep water. Idly they watched the boat-train come in and surveyed their fellow passengers.

"Here comes B-P," said someone, and a little Boy Scout Guard of Honour sprang to the alert as General Baden-Powell came along to inspect them. "Scouting for Boys" was three years old but the bare knees and broad-brimmed hats were still enough of a novelty to attract public attention, and a little crowd collected to watch the General as he inspected the boys and pinned an award for life-saving on to one of them. "How did you earn this?" he asked and, to the amusement of the onlookers, the boy replied "For saving a policeman, sir."

On a lovely summer day nearly fifty years later, Lady Baden-Powell was sharing with the Hampshire Girl Guides a great Rally at Southampton, and she was telling them that it was there that in 1912 she had first seen her husband. "He was inspecting a little group of Scouts," she said, "and asked one of the boys how he had won his life-saving medal. The Scout replied 'For saving a policeman, sir'."

When the Chief Guide had finished talking there was a dramatic moment. An elderly man stepped out from among the crowd of spectators and announced "I was that Boy Scout," and there was a warm left handshake and a friendly chat. The man who had been the boy had never forgotten the occasion—and neither had Olave for it had marked a turning point—*the* turning point—in her life.

Olave Soames had of course heard of B-P at the time of Mafeking, and had indeed worn his portrait on a button-hole badge when she was eleven and the country was ringing with his name as the Defender of Mafeking. But it had never occurred to her that she might meet him in the flesh.

On board they were introduced by a mutual friend, who doubtless thought that the General's three good-looking young A.D.C.s might be useful dance partners for Olave.

Her diary recorded on January 5th 1912—two days after they had sailed:

Make friends with Daisy Goodwin, daughter of Albert Goodwin the painter. Also Lieut-General Sir Robert Baden-Powell, the "Boy

Scout" who is so nice. He talks so nicely about Mafeking and all his interesting experiences and is so modest and sweet.

Jan. 9th. Big Atlantic swell. B-P and the three nice boys who are with him as his staff, Eric Insole, M. C. Wroughton, and Noel van Raalte, are so jolly. The latter lives at Brownsea, one mile from us. Make friends with Miss Hunt, Parkers, and Mrs Low, and organise a concert. Big sea running.

Old enough to be Olave's father, Baden-Powell was a "confirmed bachelor", who had proudly boasted to his brother officers that there was only one woman in his life and that was his mother. "Look out," they said, "you'll get it badly one of these days."

And now that moment had come. Day after day, as he sat on deck sketching everything that he saw, Olave sat beside him, talking a little but mainly listening, and learning from him not only about his past adventures but also of his future plans for the boys of Britain. He was on the first stage of a world tour to see Scouts in those countries overseas where Scouting had already been taken up, and Olave was enthralled by all that she heard. She had always known that there ought to be more in life than tennis, dancing, and arranging the flowers. Was this, then, the thing that she had been waiting for?

As they talked and walked together the two found that, despite their difference in age, they had very many thoughts and ideas in common. They even discovered that they had the same birthday, February 22nd.

They fell deeply in love and by the time they parted in Jamaica they were secretly engaged. Then B-P went away to carry out his Scouting tour, as planned, and Olave stayed on with her father until it was time to return to Grey Rigg with her happy secret and only B-P's letters to reassure her that the whole thing had not been a lovely dream.

Time went by in its invariable manner and by September he was back in England and travelling in some trepidation to Grey Rigg to ask Mr Soames for permission to marry his daughter. Difficulties were of course pointed out. He was too old, he had no money apart from what he earned—and so on. His own mother, too, had rather dreaded the marriage of yet another son. Two had already left the nest, and they had always been a closely-knit family, sharing the expenses as well as the comforts of a family home in London, which might now have to be given up.

But B-P's practice, as well as his theory, had always been that "if a thing is difficult it can be done at once; if it is impossible it may take a little longer." This marriage was certainly not an impossible proposition and the difficulties could be ironed out. Having got the rather unwilling consent of Olave's parents he wrote to his mother:

Grey Rigg.

I have been wondering what to give you as a birthday present but I think I've got one now that will please you (as I hope and believe) and that is a daughter-in-law for you. Olave Soames, whom I met on board the Arcadian, travelling with her father, promises to make a very good one. I hope you will like her half as much as I do . . . I will tell you all about it when I get back on Monday—and get your consent and good wishes.

On October 4th Olave attended her first Boy Scout Rally "and we are so cheered", and on the 12th of that month "my first public performance alone. I present Shield to Parkstone Scouts and make my maiden speech."

On October 30th there was a quiet wedding at Parkstone, in St Peter's Church, conducted by the Rector, the Rev. the Hon. Reginald Adderley, followed by a few days at Mullion Cove by way of honeymoon.

And now at last Olave had left the last of her many parental homes to make a new one with her husband and to find in him the perfect partner for life.

In these days when so many of the marriages that are written about in novels or reported in the Press are the unhappy, complicated, or broken ones, and where so many children are lost and bewildered through having more than one set of "parents", it may seem prosaic to write of a completely and permanently happy union, the children of which, when their time comes, also remain happily married. But this is a true story.

Looking back on this fateful voyage one cannot help wondering what would have happened to the Guide Movement if those two berths in the *Arcadian* had not been cancelled!

Though they had met on board for the first time, Baden-Powell the observant knew that it was not the first time that he had seen Olave. During the winter of 1910 in London, when Doogie her spaniel had been her constant companion, she had walked with the dog in Kensington

Gardens, and B-P, on his way from his mother's house in Prince's Gate to Knightsbridge Barracks, had noticed the girl who walked with such a firm step and purposeful tread, and had felt that he would like to know her. Now, two years later, he still remembered the girl and the dog and, comparing notes with Olave, had proved his point. In 1910 he had been writing in his boys' paper, *The Scout*, of how one could judge to a certain extent of people's characters by the way they walked, and had illustrated his paragraphs with sketches showing various types of gait. As a keen amateur actor he had made a study of the subject and in his secret service work in the Army had practised various types of deportment by way of disguise.

And now he was going to test his wife's ability for living the simple life under canvas. So off they went to Algeria for a second honeymoon, far away from civilisation, with tents and blankets and a single cooking pot. Olave proved herself to be an adept and happy camper, ready to turn her hand to anything, and to make a comfortable home even in the desert. She came through her test with flying colours.

They travelled across the fertile plains close under the Aures mountains and explored the wonderful old ruined city of Timgad, a Roman settlement which had been carefully excavated and where, among the ruined shells of buildings, there were occasionally to be seen old archways, and a pavement as firm and well preserved as if it had been recently made.

They spent days in the desert, seeing no-one other than the occasional cavalcades of nomads, Arab tribes on their way to pitch their camel hide tents in a fresh place.

To his mother B-P wrote:

Olave is a perfect wonder in camp—thoroughly enjoys the life and is as good as a backwoodsman at it. She is a splendid walker, a good scout, never loses her way ... She looks after me like a mother, absolutely spoils me. You were so right, my dear Ma, when you said one ought to marry a young woman.

And talking to Boy Scouts at a Rally at Parkstone after their return to England, he said:

You see a lady here in a beautiful black hat and a white coat. I saw her not so long ago scrubbing out a saucepan. We were living the simple life in the desert. We only had one pan and it had to be used for frying our fish and also for boiling our coffee. After the lady had fried the fish she had to get some grass roots and sand and scrub the pot out before we could make the coffee. The lady was quite able to do it and she did it well. She also did the washing. But I must stand up for the Scouts and the mere man—she had to fall back on me to do the ironing!

And now it was back to work for the Chief Scout and time to settle down. After a few months in a London flat, 35 Rutland Court, they came to the conclusion that the country was the only place for two country lovers.

B-P had started an experimental farm for Scouts wanting to take up work either on the land at home or overseas. This was at Buckhurst Place, Wadhurst, in Sussex, and he found a house near to it at Ewhurst, a village overlooking the river Rother. Across the valley was the old Bodiam Castle and they were surrounded by lovely views.

They moved into Ewhurst Place the same year—1913—and there their three children were born—Peter on the first anniversary of his parents' wedding, October 30th, Heather in 1915 and Betty in 1917.

The arrival of a son and heir was a great event, with congratulations from many parts of the world. From Canada the Duke of Connaught cabled his greetings and expressed his wish to be the baby's godfather.

It is interesting, in passing, to compare the domestic situation in country houses of the period with that of today. Up till the war of 1914-18 it had barely changed since the early nineteenth century, and the occupants of moderate sized houses, living on moderate incomes, were surrounded with domestic help of every sort.

At Ewhurst Place there were never less than three indoor servants, including a cook, and Olave's household accounts in 1913 included a wages bill averaging ten or eleven pounds a month. This cannot be compared with present day payments because the household staff of those days had all their "keep", laundry, comfortable bedrooms and sitting room or servants' hall, and usually their uniform as well. They were on the whole a happy and contented entourage, leading their own lives below stairs or behind the baize door, and treated with every

consideration and respect by employers of the B-P pattern. If cook gave
notice, or one of the maids left to "better" herself, there was an
immediate search for replacements, as no lady of the house was expected
to enter her own kitchen except to give orders or to collect the dogs'
dinner.

It was the same with the outdoor staff. The gardener who, today,
receives thirty shillings for three hours' work, was happy to receive that
sum as a weekly wage, but it usually included a rent-free cottage and
other emoluments.

The B-Ps had hardly had time to get used to their position as proud
parents before the great war of 1914 burst upon the world, disrupting
all normal life.

As a retired Lieutenant-General B-P was not liable for military
service, but he at once offered to raise a corps of ex-Scouts or ex-South
African Constabulary officers and men, but Lord Kitchener assured him
that he could think of no more important task for B-P than to carry on
with his Boy Scout movement. Kitchener knew all about Scouting; he
had his "own" troop in North London, and he had coined the phrase
"Once a Scout always a Scout". He knew what sort of men would be
needed in the years to come and he urged B-P to continue to lead them.

In the early days of their marriage Olave was fully occupied with home
and children and took on few public duties. But behind the scenes she
was an immense help to her husband, teaching herself to type his books
and articles and to drive the small car—their chauffeur having joined
the Royal Flying Corps.

July 8th 1915. My darling gives me first lesson in driving Jimmie,
sitting beside me and holding his breath as I make—or rather the wee
car makes—squawky noises.

Heather's christening in Ewhurst church in July was also the
occasion of a grand Scout and Guide Rally on the home lawn. A Guard
of Honour of Sea Scouts and of Guides from Roedean School lined the
path from the church to the house, the girls still wearing Scout hats and
carrying staves in imitation of their brothers.

In August that year Olave paid her first visit to Ireland, and "am
fearfully amused at my first glimpse of Irish life. Walked about Phoenix
Park, Dublin, and peeped into the old Barracks R. was in years ago.

Thence to Recess, Connemara. Jolly place, lakes, streams and mountains."

On these travels B-P was busy with his Scouts but Olave was not at this time greatly interested in Girl Guides. There was a great shortage of Scoutmasters, all men of military suitability having left to join the Forces; and the troops were left to run themselves with the help of older men or of lady Scoutmasters who stepped in the breach. Olave helped with the Scout troop in Ewhurst village and in 1915 went in Scout uniform to Calais to serve behind the bar in a Recreation Hut given to the Y.M.C.A. by the Mercers Company on condition that it could be staffed with Scout workers. The Boy Scouts Association issued an appeal for another Hut and this was established at Etaples. These two Huts were the scene of Olave's activities during the winter of 1915. This experience gave her further opportunity of proving her ability to "make do and mend", as she and her girl companions shared a tiny cottage where they had to depend on themselves for everything. Life must have seemed very strange but she was happy to be able to share in a bit of the unpleasantness of war and was most adaptable. Even if her cooking left something to be desired, the soldiers who came out of the trenches to use the huts in their rest period certainly enjoyed having these cheerful young women to feed and encourage them, and to help and advise them over the many little problems that arise when a man is separated for months from his wife and family.

"You don't know what it has meant for us to have you ladies here," said a soldier as Olave handed him his mug of cocoa; and it was words of encouragement like this that made it seem worthwhile to have left home and babies and to be doing a little bit to help those who were trying to win the war.

The hardest work comes in the evenings, especially if it be, as it generally is now, a wet or freezing night. The men come out of their thin windy tents in the dark, through the slosh and sleet, to get warmth, light, and dry standing room, if only for an hour or two. They are so well-behaved and jolly, and so grateful for the little we can do to make their life here more bearable.

It is great to see the happy crowd of men enjoying their evening under this roof. Sometimes there is a concert and the hall is packed from end to end with a critical but wildly enthusiastic audience. On other days there is just a ceaseless hum of talk. The day's news is read out by the Hut Leader and this is listened to eagerly and attentively while you could hear a pin drop, though before and after it the place is a veritable babel.

As bed-time draws near our busy time begins. There is a steady move towards the urns of hot drinks and we have to "hustle some" until the dreadful moment when the lights are put out and reluctant buyers are sent away by reluctant sellers.

And then we splosh back to our little cottage, made happy by the thought of the friendly little chats one has had—words of no great meaning perhaps but with a world of good fellowship in them.

All the long-hidden abilities and potentialities of this hitherto cushioned girl were now showing themselves as occasion arose; and she proved herself undaunted by the dreary discomforts of life in war-ridden France, no less undaunted than she had been in their camp in the desert.

B-P was frequently over in France, giving lectures, and paying visits to his regiment in the front line, and he was able from time to time to visit the Huts, to talk to the men, and even to give a hand behind the bar.

So the winter of 1915 wore on, and Olave stayed on in France longer than she had intended, waiting for reinforcements for the Hut work which were slow in coming.

But at last, after a spell of influenza had laid her low, the day of her release came, and she left France satisfied that good supplies of workers were coming along to staff the Huts for which the Scouts were responsible.

It was spring when Olave returned to Ewhurst, and her two babies had grown out of all recognition while with their grandmother. After those months of mud and discomfort in France it was wonderful to be back, even though the booming of guns across the water was a constant tragic reminder of what was going on.

April 1st 1916. Glorious to be home again. Walk up the valley with lunch in our pock nooks and train back from Northiam to Bodiam. The marsh is lovely and the many wild birds a delight. Zeppelin raid and one is brought down in the Thames . . . We are very fond of this, our first home together, but as the owner has been killed and it is up for sale, we shall have to quit. We have not got capital to buy the place and also it is not quite suitable, facing north and bad train service. So we must start looking for another house to rent.

Ewhurst had been a happy nest for the babies, and had all the advantages of its drawbacks. It was real country. There was rough shooting for the Chief's gun—very important in those days of food shortage—mushrooms and blackberries in season and every rural joy imaginable. Olave had loved her village life, her Scouts and other ploys, and was sorry to go, but the move was inevitable.

They had found a little Tudor barn house, Little Mynthurst Farm, near Horley in Surrey, and moved in after Betty, the youngest of the children, was born.

More home-making for poor Olave, and if it be true that "three removes are as bad as a fire" she must have endured many conflagrations or their equivalent by this time.

Little Mynthurst had the advantage of being more accessible by train to and from London, but the countryside was nothing like Sussex; the house was rather inconveniently small, its floors and doors creaked with age, and the low beams seemed to come in contact with B-P's head on every possible occasion—to the detriment of his language, said Olave!

They had not yet found the perfect home though they spent two enjoyable summers at Little Mynthurst with the three small babies.

As in the later war something was always "in short supply" and a satisfactory scheme of rationing was lacking. With three children to feed a prevailing milk shortage had its complications and the B-Ps took to goat keeping, and, for a short time, to bee-keeping, since there was seldom any jam available in England.

The war in France dragged on its weary way. Olave went there again in 1917, this time to visit The WAAC and to report on their work and conditions there.

Her experience in canteen work in France had convinced Olave of the tremendous value of the Recreation Huts for the men, and she suggested that, as the Scouts had given one Hut, the Guides might like to follow in their footsteps and provide another, to be sited in a camp where there was great need for one. The response was instantaneous, money flowed in from Guide Companies and from individual members, and the total amount raised was five times the sum that had been suggested. In addition to the Hut, and its further amenities which were later added, the Guides were able to supply a motor ambulance for work at the front, and this was presented to the Army Council by Princess Mary, on behalf of the Guides.

At long last, on November 11th 1918, came the Armistice, with relief and rejoicing and flags flying everywhere, including those which fluttered from the nursery windows at Little Mynthurst Farm.

CHAPTER V

The Guides

B-P the Scout had been studying Olave in her various enterprises, and by now he knew that she had it in her to do a far bigger job than that of assistant secretary or chauffeur. There was no thwarting—nor did he wish to thwart—those determined little girls who insisted on imitating their brothers in taking up Scouting. This was an idea acceptable neither to the girls' parents nor to the boys themselves.

So, willy-nilly, he had had to turn them into Girl Guides, with the help of his sister Agnes. Guides, he told them, were even more important than Scouts, for as wives and mothers they would be able to guide and lead their men-folk in the right direction—if only they had learned the way themselves.

It had not at first been a popular suggestion with the girls. They had revelled in their outdoor Scouting and now it seemed that they were going to be turned into nurses and housemaids, to lose their adventures and to exchange their patrol names from those of wild animals to flowers "which make no nice noises".

It seemed even possible that the Movement would die out or be taken over wholesale by one of the other organisations for girls. Perhaps the war saved it, for in 1914 any uniform was better than none, and the Guides did quite a lot of useful work and won their "War Service Badges" as well as the approbation of the general public, who had now come to see the value of a Movement which filled girls with so strong a desire to serve their country, and which trained them in ways of rendering such service.

B-P, though his hands were quite full enough with his Scouts, felt that something must be done at once to put the Guides on a more secure footing for the future. In 1915 he obtained for the Movement a Charter of Incorporation from the Board of Trade, thereby ensuring official recognition by the Government.

D

Olave Baden-Powell too—wedded at first to Scouting—had watched this struggling little body from a distance, and had gradually come to the conclusion that, if she really wanted to help a beloved and overworked man, she must try to take the young ladies off his hands . . . This had not at first been easy because, at B-P's own request, his sister Agnes had earlier appointed a Committee of her own contemporaries—middle-aged women—to manage the Guides, and this rather "early Victorian" team had considered Olave too young and inexperienced to join them. Her services, diffidently offered to Headquarters, had been politely declined. In September 1914 she had noted in her diary:

> To the Girl Guide Office, but the Committee prefer to do the work without me!

Now, however, some fresh air was blowing over the organisation. October 9th 1914: "Girl Guide upheaval starts." The old Council, reorganised as an advisory body, appointed a new Executive Committee with B-P himself as Chairman, and some more up-to-date women to run the various departments.

Olave now had second thoughts about the help that she should offer, and she decided to begin at the other end and to make her own county of Sussex a model of Guide organisation. On her return from France in the spring of 1916, Headquarters, under its new auspices, were only too glad to grant her a warrant for this, as Sussex at that time had no-one to whom the scattered little groups of Guides could turn for help and encouragement, which meant that every little detail was referred to London.

It was a challenge and Olave threw all her unbounded energies into the task, travelling hundreds of miles by car, bicycle, bus and train, in her effort to find supporters and leaders for the keen little people. "Bradshaw"—that wonderful railway guide no longer, alas, in existence—was the sustenance which she devoured almost daily in planning those complicated cross-country journeys for which no petrol was available.

It was tough work. Everyone at that time was obsessed with the more immediate necessities of war, and few had any leisure to spare for an almost unknown children's organisation. To every twenty appeals for leaders Olave must have received at least nineteen rebuffs or refusals, and perhaps one very hesitant show of interest from someone who could see further ahead than the war. This last she would follow up with untiring energy and by persuasive letters, telephone conversations, and—above all—personal visits, would draw the wavering or half-hearted into her net.

It would be impossible to say how many lifelong friends she netted during her term of office, beginning with those few Sussex neighbours. Her Christmas card list today numbers over two thousand names, but these, she explains, are "only those that I am on Christian name terms with." She collects friends as other people collect stamps or snuff-boxes.

One of the first people to be annexed was Mrs Mark Kerr, wife of the Admiral and an old friend of B-P.

17th September 1916. Home to Ewhurst. Find Mrs Mark Kerr and Miss Nugent staying here. Mrs Kerr consents to be London County Commissioner and she will be very useful.

In the early days when, with the help of his sister, B-P had been trying to get the Guides organised, Mrs Kerr had given him a helping hand, and now he felt that if she could be induced to take on London its future would be assured. She had come unsuspectingly to spend a weekend at Ewhurst, was charmed with Olave, who owns to having been a little afraid of her, and had many reminiscences to exchange with B-P. She had a quick, almost abrupt manner of talking, was very efficient and not inclined to suffer fools gladly. She had a large acquaintance in London, knew the Founder's ideas, had had experience with Guides, was a wonderful linguist and had many other gifts and talents which could be put to good use—if only she could be caught. The B-Ps set out to woo her, and on the Monday morning, when she was due to leave, a voice was heard outside the bathroom door—"Rosie, the Chief wants you to be Commissioner for London. Do say that you will." After some hesitation she agreed, perhaps because she felt that she would get no breakfast until she did—and her acceptance was certainly one of the best things that ever happened to the Guides. She become Olave's right-hand helper and before long had the whole of London—where the Guides were fairly numerous—organised and ready for development on a big scale.

Olave herself was Commissioner for Sussex only, but travelling round even a single county under war-time conditions was not easy. Some entries in her diary at that time refer light-heartedly to some of the difficulties but speak also to some successful work.

11th April 1916. Decide to start Company of Girl Guides here.
21st June. Jimmie (small car) had several punctures.
30th July. Finish writing my pamphlet and hints for Girl Guide work in Sussex. It might be useful perhaps in other counties too.
4th August. Start early in tedious train to lunch with Norfolks at Arundel Castle. Duchess consents to be President of Sussex Guides. Kind nice people.
"My" Sussex is moving and I have caught some good people to work in several centres.
Jimmie had three punctures before starting, or trying to start, for Bexhill. So I can't go.

In October that year Olave was appointed Chief Commissioner for the Guides, by the unanimous request of all the Commissioners present at a Conference at Matlock. Her success in organising her own County had been so notable that she had won her spurs, proved herself, and was given a mandate to do for the rest of Great Britain what she had done for Sussex. And no-one seemed to have the slightest doubt that she could do it. She seemed to have been born for the task. Her success as a "persuader" was phenomenal. Of one town she commented:

They have raised twenty-seven Companies of Guides since I spoke to what I thought was a useless audience. My post has begun to be pretty heavy and I have certainly taken on quite a big job.

Katharine Soames must have been something of an organiser, for she seems to have managed all those successive homes, her many removals, the care of other people's property, her temperamental husband, her staff and her children with the minimum of fuss. There is no doubt that some of Olave's administrative ability was inherited from her, for she had her mother's sure touch in finding the right person for a job and then leaving her to carry it out.

But Mrs Soames would greatly have preferred to see her daughter lead the normal life of a General's lady, entertaining his friends and satisfying herself with her domestic career as hostess, wife and mother. When she realised that her daughter intended to join a uniformed body, to speak at meetings, and to throw in her lot with "those wild girls" she was horrified. The name "Girl Guide" was anathema to her and she never overcame her dislike of Olave's work, even going to such lengths as running away and hiding if she thought Guides were in the offing. This was very distressing to Olave for she and her mother had always been very close and it made a barrier which both regretted but neither would remove.

Apart from this, the work was something that gripped and fascinated Olave, nearly as much now for its own sake as for her determination to help her husband. It gave her just the outlet for which she had always felt a need.

The reward of work, naturally, is more work, and eighteen months after her election as Chief Commissioner, she was appointed Chief Guide for the whole of the British Empire. During her short time in office the number of Guide Commissioners had risen from a hundred and sixty to three thousand and every County had its complete organisation.

Determined to do her job thoroughly Olave would never have been content to carry out her official duties without a close knowledge of Guiding in all its many aspects. The Movement had been in existence for two years before it came to her notice; and as a child, when she would have revelled in all its activities, it had of course not existed; so now, as a grown-up, she must begin at the beginning. In order to know whether a knot was correctly tied she must "learn her knots"; she must be able to spot an incorrectly placed bandage; and in order to be able to read messages signalled to her by Guides she must study her Semaphore and Morse codes. So in these early days of her Chief Guide-ship one finds such entries in her diary as "Lesson in knots from Mrs Eggar" (the local Commissioner). She must indeed be able to answer questions on all the technicalities, as well as the principles, of Guiding. Much of this of course she could get from the man who had designed it all, and much she was herself busy designing, but she lost no opportunity of picking the brains of those who had been "in it" from the beginning.

Busy as he was with his Boy Scouts, B-P had still found time to write and illustrate a new Handbook for the girls, to take the Chair at

Committee meetings and to obtain for the Movement a Charter of Incorporation. But he could now hand over much of the responsibility to his wife, as Vice-Chair, and to those helpers whom she was bringing in every day to strengthen and build up the work.

Guiding was now being taken more seriously and with the war nearing its end many people who had served in the Women's Forces came in to continue their service by helping to train on the rising generation. It speaks much for Olave's personality that several people who had held high rank during the war were now willing to serve under this much younger leader.

On becoming President in 1920 Princess Mary was anxious to be properly enrolled as a Guide and Olave went to Buckingham Palace to carry out the ceremony. From the day of her enrolment to the day of her death the Princess Royal, as she later became, was a greatly beloved and very active President.

Most of Olave's close friends of today were originally roped in by her to play some part in the great game of Guiding. For a game it is and must always be. In all the complicated process of organisation Olave never let it be forgotten that Guiding was for the girls, that they were the people to be considered, first, last, and all the time, that "if it's not fun it's not Guiding". Therefore any plans or programmes must be arranged to meet their needs and wishes and not the other way round.

Thus, the training of Guiders (the name which replaced "officers" as being less formal) was necessary in order that the girls might enjoy their meetings to the full, through properly planned programmes where time would not be lost in deciding what to do next.

Many otherwise willing helpers had felt inadequate before training schemes were devised for their benefit and the ultimate benefit of the girls. But when the Chief Guide approached them it was almost impossible to refuse her, and her magnetic personality was undoubtedly the single factor which turned the Movement from its tiny beginnings in 1910 into the force that it is today in so many parts of the world.

At the end of 1917 she wrote in her diary:

I do seem to have got myself fully embroiled in the Guides now and hold rather too many positions. Sussex County Commissioner, Chief Guide and Vice-Chairman too. So 1917 is over and it has been a busy year and we have done quite a lot (1) Had Betty (2) Moved to Little Mynthurst (3) Matlock Conference (4) Become Chief Guide Toured Scotland and visited Herts, Lancs, Cumberland, Staffs, Kent, etc. etc.

The publication, in 1916, of the Girl Guides' First Annual Report was a proud moment. And, more useful still, the first booklet of *Rules, Organisation and Policy* was issued the same year. Compiled by Miss Thorndike (later Mrs Janson Potts) this document was pored over by Olave and its compiler, who both went to an immense amount of trouble to make it as complete as possible, and to answer therein the countless questions which the leaders of Guide Companies had hitherto hurled at Headquarters.

It was of course a very thin little volume when compared with the later editions, but these are merely an expansion of that little pink pamphlet which formed the first authoritative text-book on Guiding, and was something long awaited and eagerly studied by all participants in the game.

In 1918 B-P's new Handbook *Girl Guiding* appeared, and in the same year Olave wrote a companion volume to this entitled *Training Girls as Guides*. Published at the modest price of one shilling, this book contained everything that a Guide Commissioner should know, based on Olave's own experience. She dedicated the book to Miss Margaret Macdonald, the first Secretary of the Association, who had been the one person to welcome and encourage her at Guide Headquarters in her first efforts to be of use.

Two gifts which came to Olave early in her Guide life were the Gold Fish and her Standard.

The Silver Fish is the highest award that can normally be given for Guiding; but the Commissioners, in 1918, felt that this was hardly adequate for one who had worked as strenuously as Olave; and ninety-five of them subscribed to give her a Gold Fish—which she treasures very much and wears on all official occasions.

The North American Indians have their Scouts and Guides and B-P had long been "Spotted Eagle" of the Sarcee Tribe when, with Olave, he visited them in 1933. Olave was then welcomed into the same tribe and given the name of "Emonis-Ake"—meaning the Otter

Woman, possibly because of the Gold Fish that she wore. (When she returned to Calgary in 1955 on a visit, Chief One Spot of the Sarcee tribe came in all his regalia to bring tribal greetings. He told her that he had a baby, born the day that Queen Elizabeth II was crowned, and that he had called her "Elizabeth Regina One-Spot".)

The other gift from her Commissioners which gave Olave very much pleasure was her personal Standard.

A Standard is a large long flag, gradually tapering towards the fly, varying in size according to the rank of the owner and generally divided fesse-wise. It seems to have been first used by Edward III, the head of whose Standard was charged as his shield of arms and the fly powdered with fleurs-de-lys and lions. (*Encyclopaedia Britannica*)

The Standard to be sette before the King's pavilion or tente and not to be borne in battayle, to be in length eleven yards.
(Sixteenth Century MS in British Museum)

Colours have always played an important part in the Scout and Guide Movement—perhaps the Scouts took something of this from their soldier-founder, and the Guides in their turn from the Scouts.

The Founder believed in a certain amount of ceremonial as having a unifying effect and emphasising the fact that, though Guiding is a game, it has its religious and serious basis, its Promises and Laws to look up to and live up to. Guide flags and Standards, carried in procession or used with simple ceremonial as rallying points, certainly lend dignity, colour and significance to any event.

Most counties, and many divisions in Great Britain, possess their Guide Standards—with geographical emblems as well as Guide ones. Personal Standards are rare.

In 1922 it was felt by her Commissioners that the Chief Guide should have her personal Standard; one had already been made by the Guides in Norfolk and presented to the Princess Royal.

A Committee was formed and designs submitted from the Hon. Rachel Kay-Shuttleworth, assisted by an expert, Mrs Zigomala; and the work of embroidery was undertaken by needleworkers among Guiders and their friends. The work of mounting the various finished pieces on to their silk foundation was carried out at 45 Pont Street, the London home of the Sussex County Commissioner, Dame Alice Godman.

The presentation of this beautiful Standard, which had taken nearly three years to complete, was made by Lady Clinton, on behalf of County Commissioners and Overseas Commissioners, at the Annual Meeting of the Girl Guide Council on March 17th 1925. Its first appearance on parade was at a Rally of the Gloucestershire Guides three days later. Since then the Standard has travelled extensively with its owner to Guide Rallies and parades. Later, after years of travel, the beautiful silk foundation became worn, and the embroidered emblems were remounted on handwoven blue linen.

It is a unique possession and one of which the Chief Guide is very proud.

The Standard of Lady Baden-Powell, Chief Guide of the World, is blue (azure) from hoist to fly. Nearest the hoist is the gold (or) trefoil; then come two small hemispheres, showing a colour map of the world, indicating her post as Chief Guide. These are placed high to the left of the main fly which is divided throughout the length by two silver (argent) waves, among which are shown three ships with black hulls and white sails, four silver dolphins and the Gold Fish of the Chief Guide. Then between the red (gules) motto bands, on which are embroidered the Baden-Powell and Girl Guide mottoes in gold letters there is a section alluding to the outdoor life, showing white tents on a green (vert) field. On the extreme fly the Baden-Powell crests are embroidered.

Princess Margaret, who succeeded the Princess Royal as President of the Girl Guides Association, also has a beautiful personal Banner, which was dedicated in Westminster Abbey at the Guides' Jubilee Thanksgiving service in May 1970.

By 1918 so many other countries had taken up the Guide scheme that the need was felt for some link between them and the parent organisation, and Olave devised an International Committee, with herself as Chairman, and composed of her personal friends, each chosen because she had either travelled in, or had links with, some particular country; her duty being to act as a friendly correspondent who could interchange news and report progress or needs. It was a delightfully informal affair, started, as Olave said later, "from nothing, with nothing to go upon".

In the same informal way she appointed an Overseas Council to keep in touch with British Guiding overseas; and these two bodies were the nucleus of the great World Association which today has its bureaux in London and America, its World Conferences in various countries, and its World Houses in London (Olave House), Switzerland (Our Chalet), Mexico (Our Cabaña) and India (Sangam). At these various world centres the Guides of the nations come together and make friends, for it is Olave's belief, as it was B-P's, that those who have worked together, camped together, cooked and washed up together, climbed, danced, swum, sung, laughed, played and prayed together, will not easily, in later life, be persuaded to make war upon one another. Love and friendship between the nations, instead of fear and hate, have been one of the great aims of both Movements.

Olave is today one of the world's most travelled women and in more than six hundred and fifty flights she has covered a total of five hundred thousand miles in pursuance of this ideal.

CHAPTER VI

Finding a Home

THE difference in age of over thirty years had at first seemed to many people an argument against Olave's marriage, and it took her family and friends a long time to realise that they had been mistaken in thinking on those lines, and that they could not have found a happier couple. The marriage, begun in perfect sympathy and understanding, progressed in bliss from day to day, as the couple found that they had not only their home and their children in common but also the big task to which they had set their hand.

But one thing that was still lacking was the perfect home, and B-P was a perfectionist. Before he was satisfied they had travelled through many miles of southern England in search of his ideal. They saw many houses that were nearly right but "nearly" was not good enough. He did not want to have to move again, and they both longed to settle down in the country with a house and garden of their own.

Eventually they hit upon an area which had been described by Arthur Young, a seventeenth century traveller and writer, as "the finest ten miles in England".

It was the day after the Armistice when they came to the village of Bentley, lying alongside the River Wey, mid-way between the market towns of Alton in Hampshire and Farnham in Surrey.

With its rolling downs and grassy uplands, its fields of hay and corn, its orchards and hop-gardens, its winding lanes with flower-strewn banks and ancient thatched barns and cottages, Bentley is still a place of beauty and peace when one gets away from the road, the A31 which runs, traffic-laden, from London to Winchester and Southampton.

The little river straggles quietly through lush water meadows, and beyond it to the south lies the green forest of Alice Holt, where trees planted for Nelson's ships still grow and the wild deer have their habitation.

To this village the Baden-Powells came almost by chance. They had been bicycling round the neighbourhood, looking at various houses supplied by the house agents, and had found nothing suitable. Then suddenly, as they were giving up hope, they came upon the house of their dreams, in the countryside of their dreams, and they looked no further.

Pax Hill, or Blackacre as it was then named, stood at the top of a half-mile drive, well away from the main road. It was a red brick house, facing south over the wide Surrey-Hampshire hills, with higher land behind. On the left, as one faced the house, was a sheltered rose-garden where right on into winter the roses bloomed and pigeons fluttered to and from their little white cote.

It was the end of the first great war when the B-Ps moved in and they changed the name from Blackacre to Pax Hill to commemorate the fact. The name Pax became, in later years, a name to conjure with and there are today, scattered round the world, Pax Hills, Pax Houses, Pax Tors, Pax Wolds, Pax Woods, and many other variations, all taking their name from this Hampshire house which has meant so much to so many people.

Pax Hill became the Baden-Powells' real home and not only for the Founder and his family, but for the Scout and Guide family too, whose members loved nothing better than to call in on their Chiefs, to put up their tents on the grass bordering the long drive, and to be welcomed to a tour of house and garden.

The twenty years that proved to be the happiest of her life, in a permanent home at last, began rather sadly for Olave. That winter both her father—whose actions had always been unpredictable—and her only sister Auriol—a victim of depression following the Spanish influenza outbreak—died under tragic circumstances.

Now Olave had many additional anxieties and responsibilities to cope with in the care of her stricken mother and the three little girls left by Auriol Davidson whose widower husband could think of no better plan than to leave them in the care of their grandmother. Unfit at her time of life for such a charge, Katharine Soames depended very largely on Olave who not only took over the baby, Yvonne, entirely but also had the older girls for their school holidays, so that there were often six children at Pax Hill. It was fortunate that this move into the larger house had been made and that Pax, with its wings which were later added, was able to house them and their attendants.

These unlooked for events, just as she was getting into her stride as Chief Guide, must have put a great strain on Olave, not only emotionally but in the amount of extra work involved. But she had her husband at her side to help and advise and to co-operate in all her planning for the children, and Pax Hill was to become the happiest of homes for them all. The children who grew up there can never say enough about their good fortune to have had such a background and for what she did for them Olave has felt richly rewarded.

As the children grew, so did the Scout and Guide movement and so also did the house—by the addition of a service wing and a visitors' wing. The children had their share in all this and spent happy hours watching the builders and playing on the scaffolding. The west wing, with its large music room, was designed by B-P himself and was filled with his Scout mementoes from many parts of the world as well as his presentation swords and caskets. The bedrooms for their visitors had the same exquisite view to the south that he had from the balcony on which he slept, summer and winter. It is a view still lovingly remembered in many places for in those days Pax Hill was the Mecca to which came Scouters and Guiders from the great cities of the United States, from the lonely Canadian prairies, the African veldt, the Australian bush, from Mission stations in India, China and Japan, as well as from every part of the European homeland. Visitors were many and scarcely a night passed without one or more.

Indoors there was a continuous atmosphere of pleasant activity. The drawing-room was the Chief Guide's work-room where, at desk and typewriter, she spent many hours each day, looking out longingly at garden and tennis court which she felt should be her reward only when her desk was clear. At that time she must have written thousands of letters, with no secretary to help her. The typewriter had come into its own and she became a swift and competent typist, with a style entirely her own, and a freedom in the use of margins, capitals and punctuation marks such as no typing school could have approved but which have made her letters every bit as individual as those written by hand.

In the winter evenings the drawing-room was turned into the

children's playroom in the parents' brief time when they could enjoy games with them and share their activities. To circumnavigate the room without touching the floor was a favourite challenge, and it is not to be wondered at that Peter was heard to add to his evening prayers the petition "God bless the furniture".

If B-P was a home-lover, Olave was certainly the home-maker. Nobody could induce her to enter a dressmaker's establishment or hat shop before it was absolutely necessary; but china shops and iron-mongers invariably attracted her, and in the arranging of pictures and books she could always be happy.

Yet, for these two, home-making was never an end in itself. Home was a place to come back to after activity abroad—and their journeys in those days were many. At home you could be sure of a warm welcome from children, staff, or dogs, and a comfortable bed after the day's work was done.

Life at Pax Hill during those twenty years was perhaps as blissful as any life on this earth could be, where work and joys were shared, troubles halved, and interests identical.

Olave might conceivably have taken life a little too seriously if it had not been for the light-heartedness—often expressing itself in ridiculous acting, comic impersonations or boyish clowning of her gifted husband. A man will often take life more easily than a woman and, brilliant as his brain undoubtedly was, and hard and conscientiously though he worked, he invariably made time for refreshment and exercise through games and fun with the children, walks with the dogs, fishing, sketching, and occasional visits to cinema or theatre. And, through his earlier life of soldiering he still had many outside interests and duties to keep in touch with.

To uproot Olave from her desk and make her join in ordinary frivolities was for him almost a daily task, for he realised that women, if left alone, are apt to become one-track-minded, and so eventually less fitted for a big job. Olave would seldom have been content to play games, to play her fiddle, or otherwise to refresh herself before her desk was clear had it not been for her persuasive husband. He had no such qualms; his own desk was always piled up with work and he would often leave a strenuous task or thought-provoking problem to go fishing —to find that in the interval things had sorted themselves out.

Wet or fine, busy or less busy, he would drag her out for exercise; she might start out reluctantly, worrying over problems left behind, but return later to her desk refreshed and invigorated, and often with the answer to some knotty point sizzling in her mind ready to be translated into action.

Olave was, and is, par excellence an organiser, and she knows it. "I love making plans," she will say, and "what I am good at is making suggestions and getting other people to carry them out."

In those years between the two wars she had proved this up to the hilt. Anyone who had tried unaided to turn a few Guide workers into many thousands in the space of four years would have given up the struggle. It was her capacity for finding the right person, "charming" her into the Movement and then leaving her to get on with the job that did the trick.

She was buoyed up of course by the steady growth and development of Guiding under her hand, and by the number of enthusiastic helpers that she was able to gather into her net. Her deputies for the various parts of the British Isles were already taking some of the work off her hands and as each county completed its organisation she could mark it off on her large map as "something accomplished, something done".

There was a fashion in the early twenties for "bobbed" or "shingled" hair; and Olave, whose heavy mane had always been a burden to her, longed to cut it short. To Mrs Mark Kerr she said mournfully one day: "The Chief says I am not to cut my hair off until every county in England has been organised—I suppose that means never!" In 1920 the last of the English counties had acquired its "independence" but Olave has kept her long hair till today.

In 1922 Dame Katharine Furse came in to help her as Assistant Chief Commissioner; and three years later Lady Delia Peel took over the responsibility of Chief Commissioner, Olave handing over to her a completely organised and happily functioning affair.

But her work as Chief Guide still kept her busy from morning till night. She had to be "in" on everything and this meant Conferences and Committees, meetings and tea-parties for leaders, and for the Guides themselves rallies, rallies, rallies, every weekend throughout the summer months. But however busy and however long the journey, she always made an effort to get to Pax in time for nursery tea on Sunday.

In her country home all times of the year were a joy to Olave; Spring with the sap bursting in the trees and expeditions to the woods for primroses; Summer with fishing picnics by the river, gardening and tennis; in the Autumn mushrooming and blackberrying in the fields behind the house—and in the winter "ride-walks" with the children on their ponies through the lovely Hampshire countryside. Dogs, too, were a great asset in that they must be exercised and when her husband was away in London Olave had to rouse herself from her all-absorbing typewriter to give the three dogs the exercise which was as necessary for her as for them.

"No gardener deserves to go to Heaven, he has had his heavenly time here," said B-P, and Olave warmly agreed with him. Now in her eighties she still loves to dig in her allotment garden at Hampton Court and to grow all her own flowers.

The village of Bentley will live for ever in the memories of people scattered throughout the globe, for in those magic years—1918–1938— Pax Hill was the veritable centre of the Scout and Guide movement, the place from which inspiration and enthusiasm was spread. Both branches now had their efficient Headquarters in London, with Committees to formulate policy and staffs to carry it out; training camps and camp grounds throughout the country and, later, international meeting places. But it is true to say that a visit to Pax Hill, a personal talk with B-P or Olave, was the aim of every leader, whether at home or abroad, and that what they gained in even a short visit was enough to carry them on and to persuade them of the worthwhileness of what they were doing.

Each summer there were parties at Pax Hill for the staffs from Headquarters in Buckingham Palace Road, and the young people who spent happy days on the lawn playing games with their Chiefs, eating picnic lunches and ice-creams with them, and picking armfuls of flowers to take back to London never forgot it. As middle-aged men and women they write nostalgically, and many like to visit her, just to say to Olave how they have kept up their interest, and often their active work, because of this personal touch of long ago.

On these occasions Olave was in her element, dispensing hospitality, talking to everyone and showing the treasures of the house. As the Headquarters staffs increased in number with the growth of the

Movement, two days instead of one had to be set aside, with a hundred or more visitors each day and a skeleton staff left in each London office.

As the children grew old enough to share in these occasions they learned from their parents the great lessons of hospitality and friendliness.

The local people were by no means forgotten. A couple of garden parties—then very much the fashion—were held in the summer months and there were also friendly gatherings of Bentley's Women's Institute, Mothers' Union, local Scout and Guide Rallies and camps, Brownie Revels, and outings for the Camping Club—the large lawns fronting the house were indeed seldom free of occupants for long in those golden days when the sun seemed to be always shining.

As B-P grew older and less inclined for London dinners with their heat and smoke, the annual reunion of the Mafeking Defence and Relief Force survivors was held at Pax Hill, with a luncheon instead of a dinner. This took place on May 18th—lilac time—and Olave would decorate the house with swathes of sweet-smelling lilac of every shade of purple and pink. The Bentley Country Dancers, in orange and white array, would give a display of dancing on the lawn, when the visitors would see their hostess leaping and bounding with the rest.

Olave was at that time an enthusiastic Country Dancer and, whether indoors or out, in the village hall or the Pax music room, this activity was indulged in regularly by herself, her family, guests and staff; and it was nothing unusual for some visiting prelate or colonel to be linking hands with the housemaid to the strains of "Newcastle" or "Mr Beveridge's Maggot". Country Dancing gave exercise to the brain as well as to the feet and as such was welcomed and thoroughly enjoyed.

Pax Hill was conveniently situated for overseas visitors who in those days so often arrived by ship at Southampton. Many of these, who had entertained the Chiefs in their own homes, would break their journey in order to sleep for a night or two under this friendly roof.

One of these visitors summed up her impressions in a South African newspaper:

Such a typical English home it is, so friendly and welcoming and peaceful looking, set in lovely country with lots of trees, hedges and

E

lanes, pleasant meadows and farmlands . . . upstairs the bedrooms all have a lovely view across the countryside to the Surrey hills. The Chief Scout sleeps out under the wind and stars and a visitor will have to be astir early to see him and Olave set out together for their early morning walk . . . I left Pax Hill feeling that here is truly the very hill of peace—a perfect place for its owners to return to after a strenuous round of duties. My memory of those few days is all of roses and sunshine and the sort of joyous peace which God sends to a home where only selfless loving-kindness, sincerity and goodwill abound.

CHAPTER VII

Double Harness

THE Baden-Powells had not been in their new home for many weeks when an urgent call came for them to go to the United States. Mrs Low, American by birth but with homes in England and Scotland, had been a passenger in the *Arcadian* on that fateful voyage when the B-Ps met. She was then on her way back to the States to take the Guide Movement to the girls there, having met the Founder in London and been deeply impressed by his ideas. Now, seven years later, the Movement was going ahead in America though, oddly enough, still calling itself Girl Scouting —and she wanted the B-Ps to come and see it and give it their blessing and encouragement.

This was the beginning of a very big thing for the girls of the United States. The Movement had caught on like wildfire and the U.S.A. has never ceased to be one of the most enthusiastic of all the countries.

It was Olave's first adventure abroad as Chief Guide. She did not feel at all sure of herself, but she need not have doubted. From New York B-P wrote: "Olave is speaking really well and is doing great things for the Movement here."

This trip had some very far-reaching consequences. For one thing it brought Mrs J. J. Storrow into the world picture.

Content with what they were doing for their own girls, and regarding Mrs Low as their Founder—which indeed she was—Mrs Storrow, a rich and influential woman, had been a little reluctant to admit any "outside interference" and while quite ready to let B-P deal with the boys, of whom her late husband had been a beloved President, she later admitted that she had been inclined to resent B-P and Olave being let loose amongst the girls.

But they came, they saw, and they conquered Mrs Storrow. "Sir Robert" was soon translated by her into "Brer Rabbit", and to both of them she became "Aunt Helen", a beloved adopted relation as well as a fellow worker in the cause. It was Mrs Storrow who, some years later, was the generous donor of "Our Chalet" at Adelboden in Switzerland, a winter sports meeting-place for the Guides of the world.

The tour was a tremendous success, but scarcely had they settled down again at Pax Hill and begun to plan their garden, than there came another urgent call, this time from India. The request for a visit came from the Viceroy and could not be disregarded. So, rather reluctantly, the children were left in the care of their nurse, with their maternal grandmother to keep an eye on them, and the three months tour began.

Friday Jan. 7th 1921. Sailed in the *Narkunda*. Pretty nasty leaving home and these babies for so long.

Saturday Jan. 8th. The Austen Chamberlains sit at our table with the Captain, and he *will* talk politics. (Definitely not her line.)

The Scout movement in India had got itself into difficulties from which only B-P could extricate it. The Government of India had, for some reason, decreed that only white boys could be Scouts and this had resulted in some six different bodies having sprung up, all claiming to be the Boy Scouts of India and wishing to be "recognised"; and it took all B-P's tact and ingenuity to recover the position and regain the confidence of the people of the country. Mrs Annie Besant, for instance, had organised a big Scout Movement for Indian boys "rather a wonderful quaint old lady and we have come to try to join them up with ours," wrote Olave. The "joining up" took place on February 19th when Mrs Besant was duly enrolled by B-P himself and her Scouts became a large part of the parent Movement.

Olave reported that "Guiding is all in a comfy-er position but oh, such a lot to be done, and these dear people do want pushing on and helping . . .

I don't think we have ever worked quite so hard or been quite so hustled, but it has all been huge fun and every minute has been crammed full of enjoyment and interest . . . We had a lovely day off at Darjeeling and went twenty-eight miles across country, up hill, down dale, partly by motor, partly by rickshaw, partly by feet and partly on ponies. It was fun and such wonderful country all the way. I hadn't ridden for nine years, nor had the Chief and so a seventeen mile ride for a change was—well it *was* a change. The Government of

India is quite spoiling us. Our railway carriage is too sumptuous and we never have to worry about anything: and cars are hurled at our heads for driving about to see things in between work.

But even in a sumptuous railway carriage there was no let-up from work for Olave. B-P wrote:

We were up at 5 a.m. in the train this morning and got to work on our report to the Viceroy on the whole tour and its results—and got it typed off on Beetle and finished just as we steamed into Calcutta at 11 o.c.

In April there was a joyful reunion with home and babies, with wonderful flowered garlands to show them and all the Spring and Summer to spend at Pax Hill.

Pax Hill! How can one describe it except by saying that to Olave and her husband it was a veritable hill of peace. Its name spelt perfection.

Olave, who never before had spent five years in any one place, now felt able to settle down in the home of her choice, with the beloved man of her choice, her children and dogs around her, and her colossal and absorbing task which she was now feeling competent to do. She was voracious for work and never had an idle or bored moment.

In 1910 the Guide Movement had been a tiny tottering affair, its offices housed in a single room, its finances a hundred pounds lent by the Founder. By 1920 it had become a vast organisation with an adequate Headquarters and staff, a large turnover in equipment, and many thousands of Guides and leaders in the field. To create an organisation of this kind, with an ever-increasing membership of enthusiastic children, cannot be achieved by sitting still and looking pretty, and if ever there was a world's worker it was Olave. Day after day she sat at her desk, writing letters, appeals, pamphlets, books—she who had never before attempted authorship. Week after week she—a completely untrained and unaccustomed speaker—had to attend conferences and chair meetings in different parts of the country, to address large or small rallies of Guides and their leaders as well as meetings of the general public whom she wished to interest.

Today she has only to appear on the scene at the appropriate moment, to be cheered and welcomed with a standing ovation at any rally of Guides; but in those days she often had to organise, or help her Commissioner to organise, the whole affair and see it through from beginning to end. No worker in any field, plumber or politician, can have put in so many hours as did Olave Baden-Powell in those twenty years between the two wars. She seemed to have a sense of urgency in her work as Chief Guide. *His* Movement, *her* Movement must be completed, its framework firm but elastic, ready to take in the thousands of enthusiasts who were continually coming along.

Brownies, for those too young to be Guides, Rangers for the older ones, Cadets for those schoolgirls who would later be leaders, and training for the Guiders themselves—all these things had to be planned and developed once the Founder had initiated or invented them.

Yet with all this immense work on her hands and on her mind, Olave's own family was not neglected, for to do that would have been a contradiction of all Guide training, the ideal of which was to make happy homes. She was no Mrs Jellyby.

Pax Hill was, above all, a happy home for all those who lived in it, or worked in it, and for those many who visited it. However much work there was to be done, husband and wife would go for their daily walks. Olave might demur—"Just let me finish this," but she knew she would be dragged out to get the air and exercise without which she would not carry on her work so well; and from that hour of walking with him before breakfast, or in the afternoon—even if she had found no immediate solution to a problem—she would return cheered and invigorated by some amusing incident or story that he had recounted.

In the 1920s, though the search was becoming daily more difficult, there were still helpers to be found for the houses and gardens of those who could afford the current wages; and the Pax staff of five or six indoor maids, three gardeners and a chauffeur, were happy and proud to serve these warm-hearted and considerate people; so that much of the drudgery that falls upon the hostess of today was still performed by others, and it was possible to have guests without too much strain on the domestic resources.

There was always plenty to be done, though, in the finding of staff, and in arranging the household, the childrens' nurses and governesses, lessons, recreations and holidays; and this happy little family was not free from the childhood ills and infections that beset all young people.

Sudden temperatures, broken limbs, and nursery ailments occur even in the best regulated families and have to be coped with even when business abroad claims the anxious parents.

B-P himself had also to be watched, as he was very much inclined to take on too many engagements, and his former hard life as a soldier began to tell on his health in later years.

Olave herself was seldom ill and never seemed to be tired though she confessed that holidays were sometimes rather exhausting. From that delicate little child there had grown up a tough healthy woman who never seemed to have to cancel an engagement or let anyone down through illness. The free open-air life of her childhood was now paying dividends in perfect health.

The atmosphere of her home, difficult to put into words, embraced happiness and harmony, work and laughter, and a deep underlying religious sense, felt but never paraded.

On winter evenings, when there was Country Dancing with friends and neighbours in the big music room, B-P would be inveigled from his study to "set and turn single" with the rest. There were games of mixed hockey in the paddock when hosts, staff and guests had a hilarious if dangerous time. There were ponies for the children and their friends; and of course there was always something to be done in the garden. Meals, though simple, were never hurried, breakfast being a particularly leisurely occasion, a pleasant mixture of coffee and correspondence.

Scouts and members of the Camping Club, of which B-P was President, were invited to pitch their tents on either side of the long drive, and were welcome callers at the house to be regaled with hot cocoa at night or shown round the Museum by day. Uniform covers all differences of race or rank and it might well be a member of a reigning house who would call at the back door to offer his greetings.

And, underlying all this activity, visitors were usually conscious of the serious purpose of it all. A visit to Pax Hill has spelt for many people the beginning of a career of service.

CHAPTER VIII

Travelling Happily

IT must have been an unorthodox person who had the idea of inviting Olave—who had never been to school, let alone to University—to address the Conference of the Canadian Council of Education in Toronto in 1925.

Possibly the authorities felt that a little fresh air from outside might assist their deliberations. For Olave it was certainly something of an ordeal, but she was now discovering that, having something to talk about, she was not at a loss for words.

Much of what she said at this Conference of more than forty years ago holds good today, proving that basic principles of Guiding have not changed, however much the details may have been trimmed to meet the needs of the times.

Rudyard Kipling had been their near neighbour at Ewhurst, and it was to his *Jungle Books* that the Wolf Cubs owed much of their training and many of their games. Perhaps that was why Olave's opening words referred to this great advocate of Scouting, who later wrote his *Land and Sea Tales for Scouts and Guides*.

Rudyard Kipling has said that England is a garden. Canada is a garden too, and as gardeners we all want the very best tools for doing our work. Guiding is a tool that we hope you will use, if you see good in it, for helping the work that is going on within the school.

I would like to explain what Guiding is and why the Movement is there at all. It came naturally because it was needed. It came because people, far-seeing, clear-thinking women, have seen that there was something further needed for the training of the girlhood of the nation in all the things that matter most. We are here to supplement the school training and to carry on, outside the school walls, the good environment and wholesome training that is needed. We are here to help parents in giving the girlhood of the country a training in being useful and capable, not only for now but for later on.

A girl is a bundle of energy. Girls are the same all the world over and if their energies are not directed along right channels they will drift into wrong ones. They have so much vitality, such vast capability of interesting themselves in anything that may be brought to their notice that it behoves us to see that only the best is given to them to feed upon.

The Guide Movement came simply because it was needed by the children. They practically invented it because they took hold of it and brought it to where it is at the present time.

We must look ahead now and build for the days that are coming, and you have already heard, from one who knows and has studied the subject, how much need there is for training our children in health. I want to point out that we in the Guides, as well as in the Scouts, are aiming at preventing the many social evils that are here in our midst. There are many of them—crime, drunkenness, disease, ill-health, and all forms of misery and poverty and other social evils which we all deplore—and they are all preventable; and though it may not perhaps be wise to say so in front of my husband it is the woman in the home that counts most and therefore the Guides are the ones that we must take the greatest care of and see that they grow up into the sort of older girl, woman, home-maker, wife and mother, that we want for our country.

That is why Guiding has come into existence and why we are hoping that it may grow and flourish in Canada as elsewhere.

May I explain briefly what it is. It is an organisation that now stretches into every corner of the civilised world. Naturally it was first taken up in Great Britain where it started. It then took root and began to flourish in the various Dominions and Colonies of our Empire, and finally was adopted also by foreign countries, and there is hardly a country in the world today that has not got its Guide family, and we number well over 400,000 active members.

We are entirely non-partisan and interdenominational. Every person between the ages of eight and eighty can come and join us. It is entirely self-developing. We simply offer the tool and where it has been taken up by those splendid public-spirited women it has brought success and though in the early days we were somewhat on an experimental basis I can now speak from ten years experience of the value of the training as it stands.

There are many other societies for girls throughout the world; they are all no doubt doing splendid work and there is room for every one; but we have felt, and I think every country has felt, that unity is strength, and all these other Movements have, I am glad to say, held out a kindly friendly hand towards us since we are all working together towards the same goal.

We have formed our training on an elastic basis and tried, as far as possible, not to specialise overmuch in any one direction, nor to run things to death as women are supposed to do. We try to make it elastic and far-reaching and I am awfully glad to find that here in Canada all girls' Movements are working happily together.

We start our training when the child is quite young. We begin at eight with small people called Brownies. Do you remember what you felt like when you were eight? You were very very young and childish, full of imagination, full of what is known as the showing-off stage. "See me do this; watch me jump; look how I can do such and such a thing." They are very easy to mould at this stage but the moulding must begin early to insure that the child is growing in the right direction. That is why we started this junior branch, for catching them young. The activities are very childish but then we are dealing with children.

At eleven the child develops considerably and becomes much more grown-up. In fact I shall never again be as grown-up as I was when I was eleven. They go a stage further then and are allowed to wear the Guide uniform. They join the big sisterhood and can then go through the various activities which I shall touch upon later.

At sixteen another stage comes along—the romantic sentimental stage—where they are no longer children. We provide for this further development by offering more advanced and grown-up activities, and they become known as Rangers.

Besides these three branches we have been exceedingly lucky in the old country in finding that school authorities have realised the value of Guiding—within the school as well as outside it, and we have numbers of school and college companies. These girls who are getting splendid advanced education are also getting the romance and attraction of Guiding, so that when they leave school and go out into their new lives or careers, they may still go on working in the same old game—improving themselves still and helping other people.

We have had splendid success I am glad to say in schools and institutions for mentally and physically handicapped children, in homes for cripples, blind, deaf, or otherwise handicapped children. These institutions have welcomed Guiding as an efficient means of bringing new life and new hope into the lives of many. They become part of the great sisterhood, feeling they are not excluded they gain fresh hope, fresh desire to get well. Matrons and doctors have spoken enthusiastically of the value of this new help in the lives of their little patients. This is only one department of Guiding but it is one that is very valuable and one that we are proud of.

As I mentioned before, we have grown in all the Dominions of the British Empire and elsewhere and through this chain of Guides throughout the world we are fostering a bond of friendship among all the various units. They correspond with one another, they interchange visits, and we honestly think that by having this link, by having the same Laws and the same Promise, we are binding them in a way that nothing else can.

That, roughly, is what the organisation has come to at the present time.

You will probably say it sounds very nice in theory but how is it carried out in practice?

First of all, Guides are formed into Companies under their leaders, captains or lieutenants, and they go along four main lines of training.

First, that which develops character which, above all things, is what will tell in man or woman. We develop character through what is known as the patrol system, known in schools as the prefect system, where they come together in small gangs or groups under their own leaders; and the sense of responsibility engendered through giving these leaders care of their younger friends has had tremendous effect on the character of many girls. Then, through the Court of Honour, where Companies manage their own affairs, girls learn to think clearly for themselves, instead of always going with the herd. They learn to be resourceful, self-reliant individuals. A certain amount of character also is developed through the wearing of uniform. We wear uniform for a definite purpose. It develops self-respect; no-one can be slovenly if she is wearing a uniform and it helps to stimulate care for personal appearance. It is also a sign of sisterhood throughout the world. We dress alike and this takes away any feeling of difference in social standing. We are all sisters, from our President, Princess Mary, to the child who comes from the poorest slum of the world's poorest city.

The second line is handcraft—and this we develop through the awarding of little badges. If you see Guides about in the street you will notice that they wear little badges on their arms. These show that they have taken up various hobbies. A girl who has a hobby will never be at a loss. The badges are awarded for work done. If *we* wear feathers or ribbons in our hats it just means that we have money to buy them; but if a Guide wears a badge it means that she has had the grit and determination to earn it, to work hard and gain it.

Third—our training in health. I don't think I need enlarge on this after what your former speaker has said; but above all we do want to see that our young girls train *themselves* in health for the love of being healthy. We lead them out into the open air, to camp, and give them jolly games and point out to them that it is their business to be healthy. They have been given healthy bodies and it is their job to keep them so. That is our line—self-development of health from the inside, not from something imposed from without.

The fourth road along which we walk is that of developing the love of service to others. This is done through training the child in her early days to do a good turn to somebody every day, so that children may learn to think of other people rather than of themselves. "Doing a good turn" may seem a trivial thing to us grown-ups but we are dealing with children and we have to give the training in understandable form. The good turn done as a child will grow into service for the community when she grows up . . .

I hope this matter may commend itself to you and I ask you to give it your support if you see that it is going to help in training the girls of Canada to be the women that Canada wants.

This address is quoted at some length because it was rather remarkable that a serious collection of educationists at their conference were not only willing to hear, but apparently received with great enthusiasm, the words of a young woman who had never been to school or had any dealings with the great world of education.

Though a strenuous tour it was not quite all work, and Olave wrote from Government House, Ottawa:

> We have had the most joyous experience of a wonderful sleigh drive right away into this big open Park through the dazzling sparkling snow. I have never enjoyed anything more and the air, though freezing, doesn't feel cold but just invigorating and wonderful. I really just loved that, it was so unexpected, they don't usually have snow quite as late as this, but the whole country is covered with it, feet deep. We shall spend Sunday at Niagara as we must see the Falls again.
>
> The Byngs are awfully kind and nice, and the atmosphere is much homelier than when we were last here with the Devonshires—or it may be that we are more broken in to the ways of Governors after our time in India!

When a long journey to Africa loomed before the B-Ps, a tour that would keep them out of England for several months, they decided that they just could not bear another long separation from the children.

There were two alternatives: first to forego the journey—but that would never do, it was a critical moment for the Scouts in South Africa and their help was needed: secondly, to take the children with them—and that was what they decided to do.

It was a joyous decision for the children. Peter was snatched from his preparatory school, Heather and Betty threw lessons to the winds, and the whole family sailed for South Africa in the Autumn of 1926. To B-P, who had spent so much of his happy soldiering life in that country it was like returning home—with the added joy of being able to show his old haunts to Olave and the children.

On arrival at Cape Town the three were despatched to schools while their parents carried out a long tour of the Rhodesias and the Union. From Sunrising, Bulawayo, Olave wrote on 11th October:

> We are having such a wonderful time. It is all ripping and we have just had such a delightful time at the Falls. We had a picnic in the middle of the Zambesi, and the Chief fished in it for tiger fish, and

those four hours have rested us like anything. We are in clover here with this most charming house to ourselves. It is a sort of Government Rest House, comfy and delightful . . . Scouting and Guiding is very wonderful up here. They travelled for days and nights to get to the camp at the Falls to see us and are so plucky, as of course it *is* difficult . . . The children are all flourishing and happy at their schools and we are all looking forward tremendously to the Christmas holidays.

Gordon's Bay was the scene of those long-to-be-remembered Christmas holidays. The children paddled and bathed and made sand-castles. The father relaxed and sketched—a water-colour by him of the children on the beach hangs today in the drawing-room at Hampton Court—and Olave played happily on the typewriter, without which she never felt quite at home.

We are right on the sea and have the most heavenly view of Table Mountain and all the Cape Peninsula across the Bay. We could not have found a more ideal spot as, though we are right away from everything, there is a good little Hotel five minutes walk away, and tradesmen call every morning, so food comes and we are comfy and yet have the fun of feeling like camp. The Chief is picking up already and we *are* so happy.

But holidays come to an end and by February they were hard at work again. The tour had been successful beyond their hopes but exhausting beyond their expectations.

I am leading a dog's life, trying to get through letters in the midst of public meetings, rallies and interviews. Pax will be lovely in April.

From that time onward Olave's children saw a good deal more of the world than was the lot of most children, and geography became not a bore but a pleasure when they found themselves visiting the places which hitherto had been only names.

On their return from South Africa Peter went to his father's old school, Charterhouse, and had to stick to school work but the girls had another delightful trip with their parents when in the *Duchess of Richmond* they visited Teneriffe, Sierra Leone, Dakar, Tangier and Lisbon.

CHAPTER IX

Building Up

IT is interesting to note how the Guide Movement followed on the tracks of Scouting from the very beginning and in so many ways—mainly due of course to the close co-operation of the respective Chiefs. This was undoubtedly the case with their training schemes for leaders.

In 1919 Gilwell Park on the borders of Epping Forest—the gift of a Scout Commissioner in Scotland, Mr de Bois Maclaren—had been opened as a training camp for Scout leaders and a camping ground for the Boy Scout movement.

Three years later Foxlease Park, the property of an American lady, Mrs Archbold, was offered as a gift to the Guide Movement. Right on the edge of the New Forest, Foxlease seemed to Olave and others to be the ideal place for the training of Guiders; the house with its beautifully proportioned Adam rooms, its ten bathrooms, its lovely gardens, picturesque old barns and out-houses, its sixty acres of grounds and the whole Forest at its doors for Nature study, tracking, camping, and other Guide activities. It was indeed a magnificent offer.

But the question of upkeep was another matter. Would the Guides ever be able to afford the maintenance of so large a place? Olave was perturbed and in two minds about it.

She was in bed at Pax Hill with one of her rare attacks of influenza when the telephone bell rang. She was wanted by Lady Mary Trefusis, and the outcome of the conversation was that Mrs Archbold's generous offer was accepted. The place, with "Princess Mary House" added to its title, was to be maintained by a generous gift from Princess Mary's wedding present from the Marys of the Empire—together with half the proceeds from the exhibition of her wedding presents—ten thousand pounds in all.

In that way Foxlease became—and has continued down the years to be, a true home of Guiding, just as Gilwell is for the Scouts. It was a matter of no surprise to the Baden-Powells—so used were they by this time to such coincidences—to discover that Foxlease had at one time been the property of one of B-P's great-uncles, Mr Weyland Powell.

Training of leaders had long been recognised as a need throughout the Guide Movement. Olave herself felt that her work would have been easier if she had had some sort of initial training, and she had always fully appreciated the value of the local "trainings" arranged by Agnes Maynard, Alice Behrens, and others who had served long in the Movement and were experts in the knowledge of B-P's ideas and methods. Such trainings had of necessity been sporadic and limited, and now they were to have this much-needed centre where diffident would-be Guiders, as well as those already in the field, could go for a week or a long weekend to learn the rudiments of their work, to meet those confronting the same problems as themselves, to interchange ideas, games and methods, and to realise the immense potentialities of Guiding where properly carried out.

There has never been anything complicated about the training, whether for leaders or for Scouts and Guides. The B-Ps were both simple people who liked to use plain language shorn of "psychos" and "isms", language which would be understandable by all and as direct as their methods. Nothing was ever introduced into Guiding until the need for it had been felt. Thus, Rangers for the older girls, Brownies for those too young to be Guides, and now training for their leaders, were all brought in to meet a felt need and to make everyone's task easier. They were not things imposed from above.

Training at Foxlease started right away, under the direction of Alice Behrens, as Guider-in-charge, and with an eager band of experts in various lines. Diplomas were given to successful trainees; and from that day forward Foxlease has continued to be an essential part of Guiding. Other centres followed, for those too far from Foxlease, and the North of England, Wales, Scotland and Ireland were soon to have their central training camps.

During and after the first world war a need had been felt to find out how the Guides in other countries were faring, and in 1918 Olave had devised the simple scheme of appointing, among her personal friends, people who had knowledge of, or had been in touch with, various countries, as "foreign correspondents". This had required no consti-

At home at Pax Hill, 1925

With the family at Pax Hill

1932

At the World Jamboree, Holland, 1937, with Hubert Martin, first World Scout Director and Dame Katharine Furse, first World Guide Director

Pax Hill, Bentley, where for twenty years B-P slept out in all weathers

tution or elaborate organisation, but had enabled her to find out, through reports given at occasional meetings, how Guiding was carrying on overseas. And, travelling as the wife of the Founder, she had always been warmly received and given an insight into what was happening, though her actual mandate did not extend beyond Britain.

The first international Jamboree of the Boy Scouts had been held at Olympia in London in 1920, when B-P was acclaimed as "Chief Scout of the World".

This event led quite naturally to a demand for something of the sort for Guides, and to their World Camp which took place four years later. Held at Foxlease, their newly-acquired training camp, it brought together Guides and their leaders from no less than forty countries to live and work together in camp for a week—something in those days quite phenomenal.

Olave's invitation to other countries to send representatives reads rather quaintly nearly fifty years later:

Some two years ago it was suggested that the Girl Guides Association should hold a big gathering similar in character to the great international Jamboree held by the Boy Scouts in 1920. This plan did not materialise owing to the undesirability of having great numbers of girls brought together en masse before the public eye . . . It is thought that the time has come when Guides and Guiders from all parts of the world will like to meet together for a friendly happy gathering, to get to know one another and to see and to learn how the work of the great sisterhood is progressing in different lands . . . I wish to extend a very warm invitation to you to be with us and hope that some of your Guides and Guiders may be able to come with you.

They came in their numbers. The camp—with Olivia Burges as its Secretary—was an immense success and was the origin and fore-runner of the international camps which today take place here, there and everywhere.

And so the idea of world friendship through Guiding developed. A Movement devised for British children had caught on to such an extent in other countries that the haphazard "international" and "imperial" councils which Olave had devised developed by the desire of all concerned, into the "World Association of Girl Guides and Girl

F

Scouts" which is today quite a formidable international body with its
bureaux in London and New York, its triennial Conferences in various
countries and its succession of able Directors. The first of these to hold
office was Dame Katharine Furse, through whose timely help the
Association was set on its feet for the big work ahead of it.

But that was still to come. The first World Camp had at any rate
shown how trivial were the differences among young people the
world over, and how easily they could all become friends, given
the opportunity. Olave recognised this in her farewell message to the
campers:

> So ends the World Camp, but we who have taken part in it know
> that it is not an end but only a beginning, the beginning of many
> friendships, a beginning of closer co-operation between the girls of
> all nations, a beginning to an era of peace and goodwill.
>
> We have seen during this week the brown of Finland, the light
> blue of Switzerland, the grey of Poland and Palestine, the white of
> Malta and Ceylon, the khaki of America and India, and our own
> dark blue, meet and mingle harmoniously together under the trees at
> Foxlease.
>
> So let us recognise that there is a place for each nation in the
> commonwealth of the world and that each of her countries has its
> part to play in her walk through life.
>
> Each of us leaves the World Camp filled with a fresh inspiration
> to go forward and achieve more and yet more good for the lives of
> others while practising the Guide spirit in our own lives wherever
> we may be placed. We go from it with a greater understanding of,
> and friendliness for, other nations, with a deeper love of our own, and
> a determination to help the Guides of our own country to become
> worthy members of this great family which is trying to bring about
> "the coming of the Kingdom".

It was not until the World Conference, at Parad in Hungary, in 1928,
that the decision was finally made to establish a World Bureau in
London and a World Association which meant the end of the informal
bodies which had done their work so well, starting, as Olave had said,
"from nothing with nothing to go upon". These now willingly made
way for the more official body.

With all these complicated international commitments and the care of the British Guides, Olave did not allow her own family to suffer neglect.

1928 has been quite a busy year, but not so many long journeys or visits as it has largely been taken up with coping with our children. But it included camping tours with them in Wales and to Gilwell and for us a trip to Hungary for the World Conference, and a look-in on Austria and Germany, Ireland and Wales, and visits to Cambridge, Cornwall, Devon, Herefordshire, Shropshire, Yorkshire, Somerset, Hants and Hunts.

Peter was now at Charterhouse, and the girls busy with school work, first at home with their governess, Miss Penicuik-Clerk (Penny) and later at their boarding-schools. Heather went to St James's, West Malvern, and Betty was for a time at Westonbirt before following her sister to St James's, where the headmistress, Alice Baird, had long been a Guide Commissioner and an old friend of the family.

It was heart-breaking leaving them again when in 1931 a "World Tour" had been requisitioned, but at the Sixth World Conference at Foxlease in 1930 Olave had—much to her surprise—been unanimously elected "World Chief Guide" and she felt it incumbent on her to go and look at her larger family of "children" in the Overseas Dominions.

Admiral and Mrs Thesiger (the Commissioner for Sea Scouts and his wife) stepped into the breach and gave a happy home to the children during their holidays as the B-Ps did not feel justified in again uprooting them from their schools.

Pax Hill was let. Colonel Le Breton accompanied B-P as Staff Officer, and the six months spent in Australia, New Zealand and South Africa were filled with colour and incident as well as much hard work.

It is all being very nice and *most* worth while for the two Movements here, which have got such a boost that they will hardly get over it for a life-time. They have made money too out of our visit and we are pleased to have been of definite material benefit. Adelaide took £1,060 at the door of the Guide Exhibition which lasted for four days and the Scout Rally at Melbourne took £930 at the gate.

B-P was busy on board ship writing his autobiography (*Lessons from the Varsity of Life*) which meant that Olave was kept busy typing rough drafts to be sent home in batches.

Meantime, in London, the new Girl Guide Headquarters in Buckingham Palace Road had been opened by Her Majesty the Queen. This had been built through the combined effort of Guide folk everywhere, some giving doors, some windows, some just "a brick". One Brownie caused some amusement by arriving with a real brick in her hands as her contribution.

Heather, imported from school for the occasion, was the only member of the family to be present at the opening when Queen Mary looked into every nook and corner of the building and afterwards presented a cupboard to replace one which she had felt to be inadequate.

In 1932, to the great joy of Guides and Scouts everywhere, Olave was created a Dame Grand Cross (G.B.E) of the British Empire. She had never thought of any reward, having been quite content to shine in the reflected glory of her husband, but she had certainly earned this recognition for the long years of unstinting work that she had given to the Guides on top of all her home duties and responsibilities.

In the summer holidays of that year, the whole family went to Switzerland for the opening by Olave of "Our Chalet", the house at Adelboden presented to the Guides by Mrs Storrow, as an international meeting place.

B-P reported:

> Olave is very busy of course with the World Committee each day but is otherwise taking it easy and making holiday of it (largely because we left the typewriter at home). The youngsters thoroughly enjoying life here.

In the spring they had visited Malta and Rome where they had some interesting encounters. "Tea with Marconi" sounds today almost incredible but there the great man was, welcoming them to his villa.

Olave did not accompany B-P on his visit to Mussolini where youth movements and their differences were discussed between them; but they both had an audience with His Holiness the Pope.

> I'd like to write more but must dress for the Vatican visit. I find I have to wear a black dress down to my feet so am wearing my evening

dress with a blacket velvet coat over the top, lent by Mrs Kirkpatrick.

B-P reported that His Holiness showed a close knowledge of the Movement and asked many questions as to its numbers and progress while expressing his fullest approval of it.

CHAPTER X

Cruising Plus

IF Olave Baden-Powell had done nothing else in her life she could claim to have shown something of the world to thousands of people, many of whom might otherwise have entirely missed the pleasures of travel.

The World Camp at Foxlease in 1924 was initially responsible for the big increase in the next twenty years of bi-lateral and multi-lateral camps in almost every country. International gatherings of all sorts had now become frequent and were playing a big part in bringing the young of the nations together, and in the 1930s there came into being a new idea—the Guide and Scout cruise.

These years of frenzied peace sandwiched between the two holocausts had seen the beginning of this popular form of holiday—cruising.

The Baden-Powells were always quick to seize on any wholesome current craze and to harness it to their own ends. They had much enjoyment themselves in shipboard life when combining a voyage with the duty of visiting their family in various parts of the world. Olave felt it to be unfair that they should be the only ones to have this experience, while hard-working leaders at home saw little beyond their own Company or Troop.

"How I should love to take a whole ship-load of our Guiders to see what is going on in other countries," she observed to a fellow-passenger as they jolted through the streets of Bucze in Poland where the Seventh Guide World Conference was being held.

"Why not?" said her neighbour, Miss Daisy Mander, and there and then, in the bus, the two began to work out a plan. Miss Mander agreed to undertake the preliminary work of organisation and in reply to a letter inserted in *The Guider* she received no less than a thousand replies from people interested in the idea. The next thing was to find a ship, and this presented difficulties until one day B-P walked into the offices of the White Star Line in Cockspur Street. Having concluded his other business he asked casually—"Why can't you find us a ship for our Guide and Scout cruise?" "What cruise?" was the reply, and the Company at once began to take an interest in the scheme. Eventually they decided to recall their *Calgaric* from Canada and commission her for the cruise. On January 6th 1933 a meeting was held in their office and Lady Baden-Powell was invited to submit her suggestions.

Olave experienced a few tremors—suppose she had to guarantee numbers and the Scouts and Guides could not supply enough—what about the cost then? But the White Star's representatives reassured her that she would incur no obligations. Her name and that of her husband were quite sufficient guarantee. Their men, specially appointed, would take care of everything—as indeed they did.

And now it was only necessary to settle details of the itinerary.

It was decided to visit those countries bordering on the Baltic, where Scouts and Guides would undoubtedly welcome a visit from their Chiefs. It was also decided that the cruise should be open to any member of either Movement of sixteen years or over, with any friends or relations they liked to bring.

The thousand preliminary enquiries boiled down to nine hundred firm applications. The White Star Company took over the correspondence and as the ship could only take six hundred and fifty passengers a waiting list was necessary. Eventually the party consisted of four hundred and seventy-five Guiders, a hundred Scouters, and some eighty friends and relations. That the Guiders so greatly outnumbered the Scouters was due, first to the fact that the Guides had started the idea in their journal, and, secondly, that there had been a World Jamboree in Hungary for which many Scouters had saved their holiday weeks and their available cash, and could not afford more of either.

This was to be cruising with an object. It would be something far more than the mere sight-seeing, feasting, and propping up of the bar of the ordinary cruise, though all of these pleasures would be available. But there would be few idle moments for anyone. The cruisers were divided into patrols under various leaders who demanded a great deal of them in the way of ingenuity, skill, artistic effort, dramatics, singing and dancing, games and lectures—all entertainment in fact to be provided by the cruisers themselves—and in the event this turned out to be of a very high calibre.

Olave was in her element—and on it. She loved travel, she loved the sea; she loved being surrounded by her fellow Guiders; and as she had all her personal family on board she had for once left no anxieties at home.

So on August 12th 1933, while guns were attacking the grouse in Northern Britain, the *Calgaric* with its unique cargo sailed down Southampton water on her way out to the Baltic, with the Scout flag and the World flag of the Guides flying bravely in the breeze. Adventure unlimited for these young people—and some not so young—to be travelling with their Founder and their Chief Guide to unknown lands. The doings of the Owl and the Pussycat were tame by comparison.

At Rotterdam, where the Dutch Scouts and Guides and their leaders gave the party a tremendous welcome, expeditions by bus and river steamer with their hosts were the order of the day. There were rallies for the two Chiefs at royal Wassenaar, gifts of chocolates and sweets for all, and then through the Kiel Canal on into the Baltic, to Gdynia and Danzig, where the Polish Guides had prepared immense celebrations for their welcome. To Zoppot and so to Kleipeda (Memel) in Lithuania, and on to Palanga where in a pine forest the Scouts and Guides were having their camp. Here B-P opened "Baden-Powell Street" by invitation of the Mayor, while a specially prepared tent was awaiting Olave, decked with rich hangings of hand-woven material. Carriages drove them along the edge of the Baltic, the horses travelling silently along the sand, to the spot where the Lithuanian Scouts and Guides—two thousand strong—awaited their visitors. Then followed the Rally, presentations, and the March Past the President, in which the British joined.

Latvia was the next country on the list and at Riga the B-Ps were received by the President, who decorated B-P with the Order of the Three Stars of Latvia. Here too the Scouts and Guides gave the party an overwhelming reception, tremendous hospitality and good fellowship.

So on to Estonia where at Tallin two thousand enthusiastic Scouts and Guides were waiting to receive their guests with song and dance. Olave shook hands with each of the assembled Guides, one of whom was heard to say as she rushed away: "Don't touch me, I must not touch anyone until I have found my best friend to pass on to her the Chief

Guide's hand-shake." This was not quite such a problem as the case of the Scout who firmly refused to wash the hand which his Chief had shaken; and when at last persuaded to do so announced that he should bottle the water in which it had been washed as a souvenir.

Here Olave and her husband received, at the hands of the Chief of State, the highest Order of the Estonian Red Cross for their work in helping humanity.

And so, across the Gulf of Finland, to Helsinki, to be greeted on the harbour side by the Lord Mayor and entertained by the Prime Minister and other dignitaries. An open carriage, garlanded with cornflowers and white asters (the colours of Finland) drove the Chiefs away. The little cream-coloured pony was taken out of the shafts which were seized by half a dozen stalwart Scouts on either side, and so, amongst cheers and cries of "Come back again" they were conveyed to the harbour. And though B-P never went back to that delightful land, Olave has made many trips to Finland and has indeed "come back again" to what she now feels to be almost a home from home.

Stockholm has a name among the European capitals for its great beauty and as the *Calgaric* approached it, to be met as usual by a delegation of Scouts and Guides, the ship, said a writer, seemed to be floating along on an enchanted sea. Admiral Prince Bernadotte (brother of the King of Sweden) was there with Princess Bernadotte to welcome the party to tea, and Mrs Cedergren—their daughter and a Guide Chief—made a delightful speech congratulating Olave on having originated the idea of such a cruise. The Rally and March Past—a feature at each place visited—went with the usual swing.

Apart from these exciting visits life on board was very full and very delightful. Olave lost no opportunity of making friends with everyone and every cruiser had the opportunity of at least one personal talk with her. Lectures on the places to be visited, Concerts, Treasure Hunts, aquatic spar-fighting and other competitions and a gymkhana organised by Mrs Janson Potts, were greatly enjoyed, and each Sunday a cruising Scouter parson conducted services.

And so to Oslo, the last port of call, where the *Calgaric* anchored on August 25th and where the usual muster of Guide and Scout folk were assembled to meet them.

Her Majesty the Queen of Norway joined the Chiefs' party for tea and also, in the evening, attended the massive camp fire on a ledge on the hill-side, where Guides and Scouts entertained the assembly with their national stories and folk-lore.

The Rev. H. Moller-Gassman, Norway's Chief Scout, who had founded the Movement there in 1911, led the final act on this last day of the cruise. He came forward to the edge of the platform and led the assembled party in the "Our Father" and the evening hymn—a fitting end to a wonderful cruise. At midnight the *Calgaric* sailed for home.

One good thing leads to another and so great was the enthusiasm aroused for cruising after the *Calgaric* journey that it was decided to repeat the experiment in 1934.

That year began rather sadly at Pax Hill. B-P had not been well and on the doctor's advice went into Sister Agnes's Hospital for Officers for an operation which, he and Olave were assured, would probably add years to his life. It did, but at the time it nearly killed him. At the same time Betty, their younger daughter, contrived to have appendicitis and an urgently necessary operation. So Olave had her hands full.

Peter, about to join the Mounted Police in Southern Rhodesia, sailed for Africa in February, leaving his father still in a precarious state, and Olave endured during those weeks the greatest anxiety she had ever known. There were many ups and downs, blood transfusions, and days and nights of pain and weariness before B-P took hold of life again. But, thanks to wonderful doctoring and nursing, and to his own indomitable spirit, he was pronounced fit to return home in March and even to take part, as a convalescent, in the second Scouters and Guiders cruise which had been planned for April.

The world of Scouting felt that they could never thank Olave enough for her care of their Founder and in March she was presented by Lord Hampton, Chief Commissioner, with the highest Scout award of the Silver Wolf—"Mainly," she said in her diary, "for looking after my own darling".

In the midst of all these emergencies work had to go on and she was very busy with meetings, rallies, and the care of her world Movement.

In April the *Adriatic*, another White Star liner, took six hundred Scout and Guide voyagers to Gibraltar, Nice, Malta, Algiers and Lisbon. B-P was sufficiently recovered to be carried on board with doctor and nurse in attendance: three weeks later he walked off, a new man. Though he had not been allowed to land anywhere six hundred of his followers and co-workers had had the satisfaction of travelling with both their Chiefs, and those at the various ports of call were able to glimpse him sitting on deck.

Rallies and Marches Past at each landing place, camps and excursions, picnics ashore and meals on board, were enjoyed to the full by hosts and guests, and there was at least one shipboard romance resulting in a happy union between a Scouter and a Guider.

There is no doubt that these voyages gave a tremendous fillip to the local Guides and Scouts as well as giving to many hitherto untravelled people the time of their lives.

The third, and last, cruise, in the *Orduña* took place in 1938, shortly before the Chief Scout's retirement to Kenya. The Scouts and Guides of Denmark, Norway, Iceland and Belgium were the hosts, and no happier people could have been found than the seven hundred who sang and danced, played and explored their way through Europe under the wing of their two Chiefs. Olave, with the staunch help of Sir Percy Everett and Mrs Mark Kerr, had to deputise for her husband ashore, but he was able to put on uniform and welcome visitors to the ship.

1939 put an abrupt end to all such enterprises, and those three cruises will long remain in the memories of those who shared them with their Chiefs.

By the end of 1934 B-P had recovered his health and was fit enough to sail for Australia for a Jamboree planned to take place at Frankston, Melbourne, that Christmas. With the Chiefs on this World Tour went Heather and Betty who, having acquired a taste for overseas travel, had wisely trained as Secretaries in time for this trip. Colonel and Mrs Walton—the former to take work off the Chief's shoulders and to deputise for him where necessary—were also of the party.

It was a very happy journey and the two girls were invaluable in looking after their parents' requirements while having a fine time themselves.

After visiting Ceylon, Java and Malaya, they arrived in Australia for the Jamboree. All went according to plan and it was a great success. Olave, from Frankston on January 7th 1935:

We are packed up and the tents have vanished and this *glorious*

Jamboree is over. It has been grand, the Chief has loved it. He is beaming and happy and well and looking fit and fresh and pink. We have had three days not too busy for clearing up and thanking people, and the children have *slaved*. Incidentally they have had a gay time, bathing, riding, and gadding about.

Betty, at nearly eighteen:

It's fun being back in Sydney but personally I liked Melbourne better. Sydney is the sort of hectic place you go to for a jaunt, it is gayer, noisier, more modern than Melbourne, and *terribly* American and fashionable. You have to be dressed up to the back teeth or else have an inferiority complex. I'm afraid Heather and I go in for the latter a good deal owing to the parental views on make-up, but we console ourselves by saying that if people don't like the look of us they can jolly well look the other way.

They were immensely popular, these two girls, as they typed and danced and swam their way through the long tour which continued to New Zealand, Canada, Newfoundland and the U.S.A. before returning to Pax Hill for the summer.

CHAPTER XI

Kenya

KENYA, in the thirties, was a land of sunshine, peace, and plenty.

B-P's former Secretary, Eric Sherbrooke Walker, had served during the 1914–18 war in the Royal Flying Corps (R.A.F.), had been a prisoner in Germany, and had after the war tried his hand at various interesting and exciting exploits, from rum running to coffee planting, the latest of which adventures had brought him to Nyeri in Kenya.

Here, with great enterprise, he started up a hotel, named it the Outspan, opened it in the late twenties, and invited his old Chief to come and visit him there.

It was during an African tour in 1935–36 that the B-Ps were able to accept his invitation, and both of them lost their hearts to the place. "We must certainly come back again," said Olave, and at home in England they began to think out ways and means.

Nearly four and a half times as large as England, Kenya is divided into almost equal parts, north and south, by the Equator—the most populated parts of the country being in the south.

The southern part of the Kenya "Highlands" is again divided by the Aberdare mountain range, and Nyeri lies in the valley between the Aberdares and Mount Kenya. The Outspan Hotel backs onto the Aberdares and faces Mount Kenya, with a wonderful view of this snow-capped mountain.

Some ten miles from the Outspan lies a forest salient, jutting out from the forests which cover the Aberdare mountains, and surrounded on three sides by farms.

It had been observed by farmers there that many of the wild animals who "owned" the forest came out of it—mainly at night time—to lick the ground which contained phosphates, cobalt and other minerals not to be found in their herbaceous diet. Their constant licking had made a depression in the ground, and rains had turned the depression into a pool.

Sherbrooke Walker had the brilliant idea of building, in a large mgumu tree near the pool, an "annexe" to his hotel. This he named "Treetops", and in the years that followed many hundreds of visitors to the Outspan were escorted by Sherbrooke Walker and his wife, Lady Bettie, to spend a night at Treetops, this unique little observatory for watching the wild life of the forest in its natural surroundings.

Treetops became famous in the years that followed. It was on February 5th 1952 that Her Royal Highness Princess Elizabeth and the Duke of Edinburgh were spending the night there, enjoying the wild life at the foot of the tree, while at Sandringham in England King George VI, after a day out shooting, was dying quietly in his sleep and his daughter succeeding to the throne of England.

This strange circumstance, of course, brought world fame to the little tree house, and to the animals that visited the pool.

Two years later, at the time of the Mau-mau terrorists, Treetops was destroyed by fire, and by 1957 Sherbrooke Walker had designed a new and much more elaborate building to take its place.

Today Treetops is certainly one of the most successful ventures in all the world of big game, and each year it attracts over five thousand visitors from all parts of the world. In its enlarged state it can house sixty-eight visitors, as well as a hostess and a hunter.

It is sometimes possible to see, from Treetops, as many as three hundred elephant in the pool at one time—or perhaps twenty rhino keeping the elephant at bay.

Playing around among the large animals, and amusing the onlookers with their merry antics, is a resident troop of baboons, who have been encouraged to stay there in order to reassure the larger animals that it is safe for them to leave their forest cover.

For every tourist, naturalist, and photographer of wild life, Treetops is a most popular resort, and not without its excitements. A governor of Kenya, on his way there, had to shin up a tree to get out of the way of over two hundred elephants.

But much of this history was still in the future when B-P wrote his first impressions of the place, in 1935, to his secretary at home.

He (Walker) has made a perfectly lovely place of the Outspan, carved out of the wilderness in nine years. A line of stone-built

little suites, each bedroom with its bathroom and cupboards, wood
fire, electric light, hot and cold water, deep verandah, and a glorious
view of the snow mountain, Mount Kenya. A central dining-hall,
lounge, shop, billiard room, squash court, golf links, etc. A wonderful
kitchen garden where he can grow all English vegetables and fruit as
well as tropical. A lovely climate at 6,000 feet. Eric has a charming
wife and two perfectly lovely little daughters ... Then he has this
wonderful annexe in the shape of a wooden bungalow which he has
cleverly built up in a tree ten miles distant from here. Heather and
Betty are staying there tonight with Lady Bettie. Olave and I were
there two nights ago with him and had a perfectly wonderful time of it.
Although we saw eleven rhino no elephants came along, though last
night a herd came and wallowed in the mud right at the foot of the tree.

The place fascinated both B-P and Olave, and in 1937 they were
back there, planning for a little cottage for their permanent use to be
built in the grounds of the Outspan.

They would call it "Paxtu," "Paxtoo," or "Pax for Two," to remind
them of Pax Hill.

What a wonderful place it would be, thought Olave, for her beloved
man to retire to when that time came; where in the sunshine, warmth
and peace of Nyeri, and with no urgent calls upon his time, he would be
able to sketch and read, write and paint, and go fishing—all the things
in fact which his busy life as Chief Scout made little allowance for. Here,
too, he could stalk with a cine-camera the wild animals and birds, which
he no longer had any desire to shoot, to his heart's content.

Here, with the children settled in homes of their own, the two of them
could rejoice in a second honeymoon.

"The Nearer you are to Nyeri, the Nearer you are to Happiness,"
wrote B-P, in poetic mood, to the Scouts at home. A lovely dream,
which might one day come true. But that time was not yet: there was
still work to be done.

1936 had been a very busy year for Olave, both in her official and
domestic roles.

The Guides' World Conference in Sweden had gone with a swing.

The whole arrangements for this Conference had been absolutely
superbly made by these kind, capable Swedes, who had thought of

everything for our comfort and happiness. The Swedish Guide Association has a group of perfect hostesses . . . I have been seeing a lot of Prince Gustav Adolf here, and his charming little wife has not only passed her second-class test as a Guide at their "Foxlease" but has come to this Conference all the time, attended all the functions, and gave us a lovely tea-party at the Palace . . .

One thing which will always remain vividly in my mind was the "Guides' Own" which took place on the last day in the little white-washed village church at Rättwik, where Guides and Guiders joined together in their little service of thanksgiving nd farewell. Dame Katharine and I each gave a short talk, and we all—old and young together—rededicated ourselves to our great task. Countess Maria Morner, who had delighted us throughout the week with her lovely voice, sang a hymn of praise; the altar lights lit up the quiet gloaming, and we all came away refreshed and inspired.

Many of the Conference delegates, with the Chief Guide, moved on to Denmark, where a great camp was being held in celebration of the "Silver Jubilee" of Guiding in their country.

How much had sprung from small beginnings. The World Camp at Foxlease in 1924 had built better than it knew, and from that date an immense increase had taken place in the number of international camps in almost every country. This year, 1936, there were no less than three hundred and fifty "foreign" Guides camping with the thirteen hundred Danes, their joyous hostesses. The Crown Princess Ingrid (later Queen) spent two nights in the camp, inspecting it most thoroughly and visiting every single tent. Her Majesty has always shown the closest interest in the Guides.

At Pax Hill that same year there was tremendous excitement, in which the village of Bentley shared, in the coming marriage of Betty, Olave's younger daughter, to Gervas Clay. Betty had met her fiancé— as had her mother before her—on board ship. Gervas, coming on leave from his job of District Commissioner in Northern Rhodesia, was due to return there at the end of September; so Betty's parents, having satisfied themselves that their daughter's future happiness was assured, made no objection to an early marriage which would enable the young couple to have a "honeymoon trip" to Africa.

after dinner speech at
sino, New South Wales,
Australia, 1958

Many physically disabled
girls play their full
part in the Movement

The Founder

Soup for the Chief Guide
at Cooperstown,
New York, 1948

So everything was hustled along, and on a lovely day in September, when the hop-pickers were at work in the fields round Pax Hill, the bells of Bentley Church rang out; the Dean of Westminster (an old Carthusian friend of B-P), with organist and Scout choir boys from the Abbey, put the matter through.

There were three hundred guests and the arrangements for their hospitality, the parties for village friends to see the presents, the packing and despatch to Africa of the hundreds of gifts, helped to fill the inevitable blank which Betty's parents felt. They had now lost half of their travelling "staff" but Heather remained to be a tower of strength to her parents during the remainder of their life at Pax Hill.

Meantime Peter had followed his father's footsteps in Southern Rhodesia and had married Carine Crause Boardman, whose great-grandfather, the Rev. William Boardman, had led a party of 1820 settlers to the Cape and there founded a family. Peter's three children were born in the country where B-P had spent so many happy years of soldiering and scouting.

And now Peter's parents were longing to see their unknown daughter-in-law and their first grandson Robert.

But before they could go back to Africa other duties lay ahead.

"I have despatched my two delicious doves to be kept in my absence by Lady Manning at Hampton Court Palace," wrote Olave in January 1937, little thinking that in six years' time she herself would be "perching" in that same Palace.

The doves, "Army" and "Navy", had been a present from Heather, and their care and companionship had taken Olave right back to the days of her childhood when doves had been among her favourite pets.

The B-Ps were off to India again, but before leaving England they planted a red oak tree on the drive at Pax Hill to commemorate the coming Coronation of King George VI.

Then they sailed away in the *Maloja*, taking with them as secretarial staff their daughter Heather and a young Guider friend, Rosalind de Renzy Martin.

The voyage was delightful. Olave played deck tennis hard and won second prize in the singles event and first in the doubles. The girls danced and had a gay time. B-P loafed, read and sketched.

G

They stayed with the Brabournes in Bombay and then went on to Delhi for the first All-India Scout Jamboree which was a great success. After this B-P went off to stay with his Regiment, the 13th/18th Hussars, of which he was still Colonel-in-Chief. There he took part in its last mounted parade before its mechanisation and his own retirement. Olave was busy all the time with her Guides.

It is tremendously interesting being here just now, with all this ferment of change of government going on. These people talk, read, think, write, and even dream I imagine, of nothing else; they are so worked up about it one way or the other. To some it may seem a madness that they are getting this large measure of self-government on April 1st, but I don't see how it could be with-held with justice any longer.

Guiding was coming on apace, and she felt that it had a very great deal to bring of happiness to the backward children of the land, and that this tour, where she had been able to stimulate and encourage the leaders, had been very well worth while. She had travelled many miles throughout the length and breadth of India before joining up with B-P and Heather for the final days of the tour.

A letter home from B-P describes very graphically their last days in India.

Another red-letter day in our lives. We four have been out in camp to see the Kadir Cup run, for three days (He had won this Cup himself in his time). Yesterday was the Final, over a hundred of us on thirty elephants, from 9 a.m. till sunset, out on a vast yellow grass plain, the whole day under blazing hot sun, wobbling along on elephants, with the excitement of watching the competitors racing after pig and in one case hunting and killing a panther. Then a thirty-eight mile motor ride home over bumpy tracks to late dinner at nine. To bed at 11. From 11–5 violently sick. From 5 a.m. till now 5 p.m. I've been asleep. Now having tea and going to bed again so as to be fit tomorrow to travel to Delhi to see the Viceroy and then on 23rd night train to Bombay. Awfully sorry to leave India and all its happy memories.

At Delhi Olave sat next to the Viceroy (Lord Linlithgow) at lunch and commented: "Though so silent in public he is quite easy to talk to and is a real hard worker."

On their return to England life was very full.

On Sunday, April 25th they both lunched with the King and Queen at Windsor Castle before the March Past of a thousand King's Scouts in the Quadrangle and the annual St George's Day service in the Chapel.

> Very nice and not a bit alarming. The King and Queen welcomed us in like any ordinary host and hostess and were so easy to talk to. She is absolutely sweet. We all strolled in to lunch at a round table. R. sat on Queen Elizabeth's right and next to Queen Mary. I sat on her left and Princess Helena Victoria was on my other side. Princess Beatrice, Queen Ena of Spain, and Princess Marie Louise were there too. The Princesses Elizabeth and Margaret Rose came in for dessert and sat by R. and me, and ate—and gave us—bits of coffee sugar.

Arriving home at Pax Hill, they found that one of the dogs had been sick in the drawing-room, and, as she took bucket and mop to clear up the mess, Olave remarked that it was good to be able to see life at both ends of the scale!

On May 10th there was a State Banquet at Buckingham Palace and at four o'clock we dressed in our finery and went to London. Their Majesties shook hands with all the four hundred and fifty guests—a marvellous assemblage of people of note, Prime Ministers, Royalties, Church Dignitaries, Rajahs, Governors—glorious jewels and uniforms.

And at last Coronation Day itself with its processions "a quite wonderful and lovely pageant", with Boy Scouts in charge of the official programmes and the proceedings only marred at the very end by rain which had held off for the greater part of the day.

After this, the Naval Review, as guests of the Lords of the Admiralty, and then a State Ball at Buckingham Palace, to which Heather accompanied her parents.

And then, at Wembley, in the presence of the Princess Royal, the biggest Guide Rally ever held—sixty thousand of them. The London Guides gave excellent shows of Country Dancing, massed P.T. and camping. Sea Rangers demonstrated Rocket apparatus, and there were speeches from both Chiefs.

In the intervals between these greater occasions Olave was busy as usual at her desk, writing dozens of letters every day, and entertaining house guests at Pax Hill, where the visitors' wing was seldom without occupants. Prince Gustav Adolf of Sweden, a very keen Scout who, but for his untimely death, might have succeeded to the title of World Chief Scout, was there with his wife Princess Sibylla, and visited Foxlease with Olave; while numerous other visitors called in for days or nights on their way to and from the World Jamboree in Holland.

This was to be B-P's last Jamboree and both he and Olave realised it—as did probably most of the people present. He seemed to gather together all his strength for the occasion, was in his element, and never spoke better. On the opening day—July 31st he stood beside the Queen of the Netherlands while twenty-five thousand Scouts from thirty-one countries marched past Her Majesty. The Queen, with her daughter Princess Juliana and her son-in-law Prince Bernhardt—an enthusiastic Scout—were present on many occasions during a wonderful fortnight. The final day was filled with emotion for Olave as well as for her husband. After each country had received from his hands a Jamboree emblem—the Jacob's Staff—he made his farewell:

> The time has come for me to say good-bye. You know that many of us will never meet again in this world. I am in my eighty-first year and am nearing the end of my life. Most of you are at the beginning, and I want your lives to be happy and successful. You can make them so by doing your best to carry out the Scout Law all your days, whatever your station, and wherever you are . . .

After the Jamboree the Silver Wedding, when, at a dinner party of three hundred guests at the Mayfair Hotel, the Princess Royal handed to B-P and Olave the lovely silver gifts which had been the outcome of halfpennies and pennies offered by Guides and Scouts everywhere. There had been a burglary at Pax Hill, when much of their silver had been taken, and this silver shower came at a fortunate time not only to replace what had been lost but also to help to furnish the new home which was in course of being built in Kenya.

In November they sailed for Africa in the *Llandaff Castle*. The journey began well.

> Gib. was great fun. The moment we had gobbled down our lunch H.E. Sir Tim Harrington arrived in his barge to collect us, surrounded by his gilded staff and complete with Admiral Evans and *his* staff. Off we went, landed against the same old Flagstaff pier and there were the usual Guides, Brownies, Cubs and Scouts, apparently thrilled to have us again. I shook hands with each one of course and then the Admiral swished us off to his house. Then he drove us in a marvellous Ford right up to the very tippy top of the Rock, and, my wig, it was a view and a half. Coming down we saw baboons—such a nice couple who let us walk quite close to them and were awfully well clothed and not at all indecent like most monkeys ... The Admiral's barge brought us off to our Llandaff again and altogether we enjoyed ourselves quite a lot.

But later on B-P got a severe attack of lumbago, and by the time they landed on African soil he was so ill that many of the plans for Scout work and visits had to be cancelled. They went up to Nyeri in Kenya where he was able to rest and recover his strength in peace and sunshine. On Christmas Day Olave wrote:

> Oh it is so lovely being here again. I adore this place even more than I knew I did. It is simply perfect and the Chief is slowly picking up and recovering from his beastly lumbago and horrid cough. It was very trying and tiring for him all these last days *and* nights and so he has been a bit pulled down. But he is well on the mend now and will be fishing in a few days, though just at the moment he only wants to loaf and sit and enjoy the peace and quiet and loveliness of the garden and the view and the warmth.

Olave had been too optimistic. The illness dragged on and B-P was not able to go and visit Peter and his family in Southern Rhodesia as had been planned. Olave flew to Inyanga by herself.

> It is a lovely thing being a Granny. Little Robert is now just sixteen months old and able to walk though not to talk, but can laugh and gurgle and romp about with the best of babies. A dear lovable little

chap who, of his own accord, flung himself forthwith into his Granny's arms and instantaeously won the affection that is his due.

Later in the year Peter and Carine and Robert joined the grand-parents at Beira, and B-P was able to see them on board his home-bound ship, the *Llangibby Castle*.

Robert was simply marvellous and you would have thought he had spent his life travelling. He took it all so calmly and he has smiled and been an angel and quite perfect in every way. Dad has gone dotty about him and we have got miles of movie film of him. How you would laugh to see us being the doting grandparents and loving it. Peter is in fine form and Carine is just charming.

The B-Ps were on their way home, but it was only to be a brief "visit" to England. The Chief Scout put on his uniform for the last time during the *Orduña* cruise to Denmark, Norway, Iceland and Belgium. With Olave to take care of him on board and to deputise for him on shore, he spent his days happily reading and sketching among the seven hundred members of their Scout and Guide family who travelled with them.

That autumn they slipped quietly away again to their beloved Africa.

CHAPTER XII

Alone

THOUGH they had left their lovely English home, Olave did not at the time realise that the break was to be a permanent one. They had every intention of coming back to Pax Hill.

> We have decided to go to England for a few months next summer and have booked our cabins on the *Klipfontein*, Holland-Africa Shipping Line, a 10,000 ton new ship, sailing from Mombasa on March 23rd, arriving Dover on April 10th.

Alas for the best-laid schemes. Hardly had this letter been written than England was at war.

It is questionable whether B-P would have been able to stand up to that last voyage. He was an old man, worn out by work and over-work, and his heart was constantly giving trouble. The compulsory stay in sunny Kenya was probably the best thing that could have happened to him. While the possibility had been there he would have felt in duty bound to go home to tie up ends and make more farewells, but now it was no use thinking about it and he drew a breath of relief. He was content to leave the promotion of Scouting to younger hands and had handed over to Lord Somers responsibility for the Scouts of the Commonwealth. Who, if anybody, would ever be another Chief Scout of the World?

Olave was still in her prime. While she grieved at having temporarily to relinquish the reins of active Guiding she now felt that her first duty was to her husband. Side by side and hand in hand they had worked more strenuously than anyone realised for more than twenty-five happy years. Now he must, on doctor's orders, hand the burden over to younger shoulders, and where he was she must be. Their family, grown-up, were off their hands. With Peter and Betty married and settled on

African soil, Olave had dug up many of her English roots and transferred them to that continent.

And now the fatal day had come.

September 3rd 1939. To church. Listen in anxiously many times during the day and then in the evening the awful news comes through of war having been declared by France and us on Germany. The King spoke to his people and it was most moving and just a grim terrible awful thing to realise that war, with all its cruelties, bitterness, and sorrow, has come again. One feels dazed and can think of nothing else.

September 19th. Stitched away at all odd moments making surgeons' masks and caps for the Red Cross. It is the only form of war work I can do here and one hopes it may help. I do feel idle though. Anyway, here I am, anchored with my darling and here we must remain "for the duration".

Kenya, a British colony, and longing to help the "mother country" in troublous times, felt uncomfortably cut off from the scenes of action. Those who could get away returned to England to join one of the armed forces, or otherwise to give their support to the war effort. Others joined up in Africa. Those who were tied—as in Olave's case—to home duties, longed to find some way of helping, and British and Africans were united in their desire to be of use.

Typical of this spirit among the African populace was a quaint letter received by the District Commissioner at South Nyeri:

I beg you to accept me to offer my three pigs to Government to be used in the war. I have kept three pigs only and I am wanting them to be in the work of your Crown, according to my love and power, like other fellows who have given up their lives in order to defend other peoples lives. I felt heartedly that I have no knowledge of any work except these pigs, which I decided I must give them to Government exactly as I would give up my life for our Kingdom. In measuring my pigs they are four feet in length.

Your obedient servant Kenoga Njeja.

In their tiny home at Nyeri, built during their absence in England in the grounds of the Outspan Hotel, B-P was able to rest quietly, not idly indeed, for he continued writing and drawing for the Scouts, published three books during that time, and painted some of his best wild animal pictures—now hanging at Gilwell Park in England to be seen by many thousands of Scouters and Scouts.

But the feeling of pressure had gone; he could work when he felt like it and rest when he was tired. If he felt strong enough to fish they would drive out to "The Bend" a few miles away, where there were pools specially reserved for him in the Thego River and where they could have their picnic lunch before returning home to rest.

In the lovely sunshine of a perfect climate he enjoyed what he described as his "third life" for another two years.

For a pet, instead of dogs or horses, they now had a tame hyrax, and this little tree animal entwined himself round Olave's heart and became a happy part of their life together.

In a letter to a god-child in England she thus described him:

Hyrie is more delicious than ever. Godfather dotes on him almost as much as I do. He sleeps wound round my neck or snugged into my arms and when I wake he wakes too and detaches himself and advances into Godfather's room to have his early tea. He sits on the bed and eats some carrot-tops or rose leaves, and then jumps onto my shoulder and has a saucer of weak tea. He drinks in such a funny way, putting his mouth down into the milk and sucking it up as a horse does; but he also laps a little and stops every few gulps to look up and taste the drink, and you can almost hear him saying to himself "This is good tea". After that ritual he dashes about the room, climbing up the telescope, jumping onto the mantel-piece, rushing at my feet and pretending to bite—and you can see he thinks it no end of a joke.

Watching and getting to know the many different birds that visited their verandah was another constant amusement, and they both revelled in their "Bird Club", feeding its members on ground-nuts, millet, crushed maize, bread-crumbs, and odd scraps of meat, fish and potato. It was not to be wondered at that the membership increased rapidly as the news of these good menus went round among the weavers and honey-birds, shrikes, seed-eaters, and other members of the feathered tribes.

And if they wanted to see something larger there was always Treetops

with its elephant and rhino and other wild animals to be watched by
night.

It is not so much the number and size of the animals that makes it
all so enchanting, but the whole feel of it, the utter silence of the
forest, the stillness of the trees and lake, the delicious sounds coming
from the bush as the animals wake from their afternoon siesta, and
the hush preceding their quiet sudden appearance from the glades;
and of course the feeling of breathless anticipation of *what* is going to
emerge and how many!

There was never a pause in the scene during most of the time we
were there—just as if one group were giving their performance on a
stage while the next one was waiting "off" in the wings to move on
at the right moment to do theirs.

Then, too, there was the occasional safari further afield, to see yet
more big game—with the cine-camera to immortalise the scene.

Here is B-P's own description of one of these exciting journeys:

So we started off, Olave and I, with our two servants in the car,
away across the great grass plain which lay for thirty miles between us
and Mount Kenya. Within five miles of our green lawns and bright
gardens at Nyeri we came on the dried-up sunburnt country which
the rains had not touched.

For mile after mile we motored slowly across open undulating
plains, with never a kraal or a tree and only occasional scrub bushes.
Why slowly? Because every few hundred yards we had to stop and
look at the wild game getting such grazing as they could from the
withered grass. Zebra were there in hundreds, their fat round rumps
showing that though the country looked bare there was still sustenance
in it. "Tommies"—that is the smart little Thompson's gazelles—
were everywhere and not at all afraid of our car. Hartebeests in plenty,
looking almost like so many chestnut horses with their heads stuck
on at a stiff angle to their necks. Oryx too, handsome big buck with
black markings on their grey bodies and long straight horns—
beautiful beasts. Ostriches of course, silly haughty birds evidently
anxious to rank as animals and jeered at by birds because they cannot
fly . . .

So remote were we from wars and thoughts of war in this land of peace and sunshine that the only possibility of disturbance was conveyed on a Government notice board close by: "Fishermen, beware of Rhinos here"!

B-P was certainly enjoying his "third life" to the full, despite the increasing pains and weakness of old age. They made jokes together about his many pills, potions and plasters. "The doctor asked Olave whether the ointment made me 'irascible'. She said 'Yes' and when he had gone we got out the Dictionary and she looked up the word to see what it meant."

Making hospital supplies was not enough to keep Olave occupied, and she worked hard within the limits of Kenya for her Guide family, and by letters and articles in the various journals kept in touch with those further afield. But now her first thought was her husband and she cared for him devotedly during those last two years together, only taking time off for exercise on the tennis court or for occasional flying visits to family or Guides.

In 1939 Heather, on leave from her service with the A.T.S., flew out to see her parents, and Betty also joined them at Nyeri in time for her eldest son, Robin, to be born there and christened in Nyeri church.

In 1940 both Peter and Betty, with their families, came for a last family reunion; and that same year Heather married John King, of the R.A.F., in Bentley church. Her parents anxiously awaited news and descriptions of this quiet war-time wedding but, like so many letters at that time, most of these were drowned at sea or delayed for many months in reaching their destination.

But now the parents felt glad in the knowledge that their three young people were happily settled for life. Of the six children whom Olave had cared for at Pax Hill in those halcyon times between the wars, Christian Davidson, the oldest niece, was the only one able to be with them at Nyeri during those last quiet days at the end of 1940, and she was a constant support to Olave. During the autumn B-P's "tired heart" had refused to respond to further treatment, and he had grown steadily weaker. Olave placed in his hands a copy of his last book *More Sketches in Kenya*, published by Macmillan, and he was just able to hold it and to realise that in spite of all the frustrations of war it had come out.

Olave now barely left his side and the end came peacefully on January 8th 1941.

He was laid to rest in the little cemetery at Nyeri, a few hundred yards from Paxtu.

His beloved Mount Kenya was shrouded in grey mist when the long procession of mourners, moving in slow step to the beat of muffled drums, approached the cemetery while the minute gun crashed forth its farewell of fifteen rounds.

Soldiers, sailors, civilians—representatives of all communities in Kenya—walked in the procession, headed by the Governor and the General Officer Commanding the Troops. Sir Godfrey Rhodes, Chief Scout Commissioner, led a mixed assembly of European, Asian and African Scouts, and at the graveside, under their President, Lady Moore, were a group of Guiders, Guides and Brownies.

So the Founder was borne to his last resting place on the green hillside facing the mountain that he knew in its every mood.

As the moving service ended the sun came out and as the procession left the grave-side the peak of the mountain was shining in a clear blue sky.

*   *   *

The Scouts have a sign—a dot within a circle—used in wide games and tracking expeditions to signify to their fellow-Scouts who are following that they have gone home. This sign appeared now not only by a grave-side at Nyeri but on thousands of Memorial Service papers throughout the world. A truly great Scout had gone home.

Hardly ever can the passing out of this world of any man have been more widely mourned. Letters, cables, telegrams, messages, from every corner of the world that was free to send them, came pouring in. Messages from Kings and Queens and others in high places, as well as from Scouts and Guides, Cubs and Brownies, came to cheer Olave in her first great loneliness.

Though for so long expected and foreshadowed, his death seemed to come to her as a terrible blow, and she was left anchorless. When the immediate work of dealing with necessary details was over she longed for nothing but death. For the first time in her life her courage seemed to desert her, and her private letters and diaries were full of hopelessness and misery, though to the Guides and the outside world she put on a brave face.

The world was still very much at war. The seas were full of mines. In many countries Scouting and Guiding had been *verboten* and had gone underground for the time being. Olave felt that her work as World Chief Guide had lost its significance now that she could no longer travel.

What then could she do? There were too many spare hours in which to go and sit and grieve at his grave-side. The Guides in Kenya looked to her for leadership, but their affairs did not fill her days, though she had taken over from Lady Brooke-Popham the duties of Chief Commissioner for Kenya.

Then help came from an unexpected source. The East Africa Women's League needed a President, and Olave was appealed to. The affairs of the League were at rather a low ebb, there was no Secretary, and for a time she undertook the duties of both President and Secretary. She bought a second-hand car, packed up her possessions at Nyeri, and went down to Nairobi to live for some weeks in the Norfolk Hotel while she put matters in order, roped in more helpers, and visited the branches throughout the country, many of which were in very low water.

The work temporarily engrossed her and her days were now very full. History was in a small way repeating itself, and what Olave had done for the Guide Movement in England twenty years ago she was now doing for the East Africa Women's League in Kenya, putting fresh life into it wherever she went. Combining this with her work for the Kenya Guides she was able to feel that she was being of some use.

Writing to Olave thirty years later, a Kenya friend, Mrs Silvester, says:

> I remember so vividly your courage and control when the Chief Scout left us and how you had the vision and determination to rescue the E.A.W.L. from the doldrums in Kenya and to start the England branch.

Before starting on this strenuous piece of work she visited Betty and her family in Northern Rhodesia (Zambia) and with her niece Christian did a little trip round Lake Tanganyika.

I had no idea this lake was so beautiful. There are big mountains about, steep rocky cliffs in places, and otherwise beautiful forest-clad slopes, rather like a Canadian lake, a Swiss one, and a Norwegian fjord mixed, and quite lovely rocky beaches.

We dawdle along, calling in at tiny wee villages about four times a day, to pick up bags of rice, dried fish, bananas, etc. brought out from the shore by more or less naked Africans in rough log canoes, and it is taking us six days to travel the three hundred mile length of lake.

During a visit to Guides in the Belgian Congo, which followed this trip, Olave had an adventure which she recounted to the Guides at home.

On the day before we left the Congo my dear old Turck (the car named from the initial letters of Tanganyika, Uganda, Rhodesias, Congo and Kenya) suddenly sat down with something wrong in her inside. It was quite a bad moment as she chose to do this in the midst of a very wild and watery and woolly swamp, with high elephant grass towering over our heads all round. It was a very lonely bit of road, hardly more than a track, and it looked as if we were going to spend the night there among the elephants, crocodiles, buffaloes and what-nots, not forgetting the mosquitoes.

However, as luck would have it, a lorry loomed in sight and took us in tow, dragging us in a most undignified way as far as the Congo border with Uganda.

It was getting late and the driver decided not to go further; and as there was only one tiny house which was filled by the Customs Officer and his family we had perforce to bed down in an outhouse shed which, though not exactly comfortable, was better than being stuck in that swamp.

When we were towed further on next morning, there was a barrier across the road to stop us, and we were told we could not come in as there was a yellow fever scare and we had not been inoculated.

After half an hour and more of explaining and cajoling, and pointing out that we could not move under our own steam, the official relented, and we must have looked very funny sitting helplessly there, and being at last towed, illegally but triumphantly, back into British territory.

Had Turck been able to trundle herself along we should have been firmly turned back into the Congo, so that her break-down was really a blessing in disguise.

But this episode gave a lot of bother to the Guide Commissioner in Uganda, because a tour had been planned for ten days, allowing me to visit all the Companies and Packs in the Protectorate at leisure; and there I was, anchored at Fort Portal, doing yellow fever quarantine, and all the dates and visits in that country having to be re-arranged.

Even this activity with Guides and E.A.W.L., which occupied the autumn and winter of 1941–42 was not enough to quiet Olave's conscience, and she had a long struggle with herself about what she was going to do.

Then in March 1942 the battle was won, and she had decided to return to England that summer if she could find a ship. "Home" she would hardly call it for "home" had been where her husband was, and his last home had been here in Kenya.

But she had had letters from Guide Headquarters in England which had at last convinced her that as Chief Guide, war or no war, her place was at the hub of the wheel and not on one of the spokes.

So in March she handed over her work as President of the E.A.W.L., and her job of Colony Guide Commissioner and began sadly to pack for a trip round Africa which would end in a voyage to England.

I suddenly decided that my duty lay in England, and cabled to say that I had changed my mind and expected to come—if there is a ship —in July. I feel a gnawing conscience that I must be in this war more in spite of being such a doddery old bird. I have been thinking about it for weeks and then suddenly made up what I am pleased to call my mind, which up till then had been weakly vacillating and indefinite. So now, having burned my boats, so to speak, I shall have to come. Every morning when I wake (with darling Hyrie tucked in beside me) I groan at the thought of it being one day nearer to leaving Kenya . . . So there it is, and one day, when the war is over, I can return to this lovely country.

Hyrie, as she called him, was the little tame hyrax which they had had as a pet during those last years in Kenya. Just as, in England, horses and dogs and doves had wound their way round Olave's heart, so now this little tree animal had been her beloved companion and play fellow and she dreaded the parting. Hyrie had caused them both endless fun and amusement in B-P's lifetime, and in her loneliness she had clung to him as a creature that they had both loved, and Hyrie had returned her affection. In his specially constructed cage he had travelled with her throughout Kenya and been the cause of amusement and interest to many Guides.

Once the decision was made, Olave did not let any grass grow under her feet. She started on a tour in Africa, staying with Betty in Northern Rhodesia, and visiting Guides in many places on her way to the Cape. Then, through a sea laced with mines, a five weeks voyage, "wearing our life-jackets even when we go to the bath" she sailed for England, arriving at Liverpool in September.

She was still very unhappy and restless. Nothing really seemed worth while any more and her one idea, and often expressed wish, was to lie beside her beloved man in the grave at Nyeri—"my grave"—she called it.

But as Clement of Alexandria had put it many years ago: "We may not be taken up and transported to our journey's end but must travel thither on foot, traversing the whole distance of the narrow way."

The months after her return to England were the most wretched Olave had known.

It is so easy for outsiders to say that what had happened was only natural—she had said it to herself very many times. If you married someone more than thirty years older than yourself you must expect to live for some part of your time as a widow—unless you remarried. She had faced all this earlier on and realised its inevitability. But none of that knowledge could console her now. Her sheet-anchor had gone and she felt utterly alone.

By 1942, as some people will remember, the war had reached a stage where there was great temptation to feel exhaustion and despair. Casualties were mounting overseas—hardly a home untouched by them—while otherwise everything was rather cheerless. Not only luxuries such as oranges and bananas, iced cakes and tobacco, but such common necessities as soap, combs, and wrapping and toilet paper were "in short supply". Transport was difficult, petrol severely limited, holiday resorts out of bounds, black-out frustrating, bombing unpleasant, finances uncertain, and at a low ebb. Olave had not come gradually, as had most people at home, to this state of affairs. She had come, just as the English winter was setting in, from sunny Kenya, a place far removed from war, bombs and shortages, to find herself plunged suddenly into war-time England at its most dreary.

She had no home to go to and no-one to share it with. Pax Hill, commandeered in 1939 by the War Department, was full of Canadian soldiers, and all her possessions were in store. It was not remarkable that for the first time in her life Olave felt tempted to let go and to wonder why she had ever come back to this lonely and beleaguered place.

After living for a few weeks in hotels and in a deserted London house borrowed from a friend, one at least of her troubles was solved by the offer from the Crown of a "Grace and Favour" apartment at Hampton Court Palace. This was, at any rate, a refuge, and it was made as comfortable for her as war-time restrictions allowed. A bathroom—not considered necessary by previous occupants—was added. But the place was chilly and dark in the winter months and there was little there to cheer or encourage her. In her first great unhappiness she had even given up her favourite occupation of making scrapbooks of her journeys —nobody, she said, would want them now that *he* was gone.

The married couple who "did" for her were not the most cheerful of companions, feeling as they were the strain of three years of war-time living. None of her children were at hand to give her the lift she needed, and she had almost forgotten how to laugh.

"I am still very restless and malcontent and wonder if I shall ever come round and find real contentment."

But B-P, the ever thoughtful, had left behind him four letters for her to study and browse over. It was the serious contemplation of these which, more than anything else, restored her to herself and, eventually, to happiness. In those last years in Kenya his loving thoughts had been concentrated on the inevitable blank that his death was going to bring, and he had written to her, over and over again, that in the carrying on of the work on which they had embarked together she would find solace, through full-time and worthwhile occupation which would fill the gap and bring satisfaction in its train.

"Be happy" was his motto and one which she must not forget.

H

Mourning for what you could not have had never been part of his philosophy.

Suddenly, too, she seemed to realise the immense love and trust which not only the Guide Movement but the Scouts too reposed in her. They convinced her that they needed her more than ever before, not only as their living link with their Founder but as herself, the Chief Guide. Her enthusiasm, her knowledge of all the Founder's ideas and ideals, and her great gifts of leadership, were what were more than ever needed in this time of emergency, and there was work that only she could do in bringing strength and support to what the Movement—deprived of so many of its leaders—was trying to carry out.

Olave found that there was indeed plenty of work for her, as Chief Guide, to do though there was of course no hope of travelling beyond Britain's shores. So she threw herself and all her renewed energies into the task. Tirelessly, through darkness and cold, bombs and blizzards, she visited the Guides who were carrying out their work pluckily and often on their own, and she gave them the "oomph" that they needed just at the time that they needed it most.

And if she still hoped that a bomb would send her back to her grave at Nyeri, she never let them know it but showed again the well-remembered smile and spoke the words of encouragement that they never forgot.

In doing what she conceived to be her duty Olave had found happiness once more and a conscience at rest.

But it was tough going, flying bombs dropping around, rallies being forbidden or cancelled at the last minute, dark slow journeys in cold and black-out, and many trains disrupted.

She had first-hand experience of the blitz when staying with Lady Clarendon in London.

The Air-raid siren went at nine and for the first time I heard the terrific bangs quite close of the anti-aircraft guns and also some bombs falling from the devils flying over. The All-Clear sounded at ten and we went to bed; woken by it all again at 5 a.m., terrific noise for an hour. Dressed in case of emergency but did not feel frightened. It was a grand new experience for me and helps to make me understand what it feels like to be in danger. To the office and then back home to Hampton Court. Raid warning there again at 5 p.m. and again in the night, considerable damage and people killed in London.

But there were some lighter moments even in 1943. Though Buckingham Palace and almost every building in that neighbourhood had "had it", Guide and Scout Headquarters were still standing and carrying on as usual. On February 20th the Army Pigeon Service arranged for their pigeons to carry "Thinking Day" messages from all parts of England and Olave was at Wing House to receive them. Among those who sent off the messages were the Princesses Elizabeth and Margaret.

And on April 9th Dame Joan Marsham drove Olave down to Windsor for a grand performance by the Buckingham Palace Guides and Sea Rangers.

> The King and Queen received us and sat with us for the show. Princess Margaret sang and acted with the Guides and Princess Elizabeth also in Sea Shanties, &c. Charming family they are.

So Olave got her second wind, pulled herself together and resolved to follow the Founder's advice and to be happy. "I believe," he had so often said, "that we were put into this world to be happy and to give happiness, and that Heaven is not something up in the clouds but is here and now if we choose to make it so."

Olave had been, as it were, in a bad dream out of which she was now awaking.

But she was missing Kenya and her many friends there more than she had ever thought possible; and it occurred to her that in this war-time England there must be other people suffering the same nostalgia for a country they had helped to make, had lived in, served, and come to love. And the idea struck her that it would be good to have, in England, a branch of the East Africa Women's League, with meetings where lovers of that part of the world could get together and reminisce, and welcome Kenya friends into the circle.

No sooner thought of than done, and she got busy forming an England branch, mainly as a social club for like-minded people who wanted to keep in touch with East Africa. And in this, as in some other of her plans, she built perhaps better than she knew. This England branch has become, in later years, a very valuable organisation for helping in the repatriation of those who, for one reason or another, have had to leave their homes, their farms, or other careers in Kenya, and to find new occupations in Britain. The League has helped them in countless ways, in finding houses for themselves, schools for their children, work and interests of various kinds, and, in cases of need, financial help until they have solved their currency problems and found their feet in what to many is a new country—and certainly a tougher life.

Starting in a small way, this England branch of the League is spreading its wings and now has its sub-branches—or groups—in London and the various counties. While continuing their friendly social gatherings the members now have the satisfaction of knowing that they are performing a useful and much-needed service in these days of African nationalisation.

To Olave the League and its affairs comes only second to Guiding in her life, and on her many trips to Kenya she is able to keep in touch with its members at both ends.

But during those grim war years it was a joy to be able to meet friends of Kenya days while carrying out her strenuous round of duty with the Guides.

To anywhere that she was asked to visit, within reach by road or rail, Olave went, carrying her message of cheer and encouragement, and without thought for her own safety or comfort.

Someone wrote to her:

It is marvellous how you cope with your work and keep going. Thank Heavens your Guardian angel knew what he was doing when he said "This child must have an extra strong constitution because she's in for some very hard wear."

Perfect health and fitness is certainly one of the best of gifts that the gods can bestow.

CHAPTER XIII

Adventuring On

At long last, in the middle of 1944, there came to a weary and worried country the feeling that, in God's good time, the war might one day end.

The landing in Normandy, and the successes which followed D-day, had given everyone fresh hope.

Olave sat at her desk in the drawing-room of her apartment at Hampton Court Palace, and gazed up at eighteen "Liberators" flying homeward bound.

What a stirring prophetic name to have chosen for these great machines taking part in the liberation of Europe, and what visions the word conjures up of the freedom that is coming to the many peoples for whom our hearts have ached for so long . . . By degrees we shall hear the full tale of how the members of our Movement—both the girls and their leaders—have stood up to their tremendous test, of the courage that they have shown, and of the steadfast determination with which they have stuck to their Scout and Guide principles. Whispers have come through from time to time of gallantry, self-sacrifice, and noble deeds, and how glad and proud we shall be when more details come to light, more personal contacts made, and more doors flung wide open . . . We know that, surrounded by the bitter dangers and ravages of war, Guides and Scouts of Europe have shown that their training has stood them in good stead. We know too what valiant service has been given by those in countries which have not been over-run but where hardships and handicaps were there in every degree . . . And so now, out of all this past heroism and sturdy effort in war, comes the challenging call to continue on an ever advancing scale in our work for bringing together the young people of the world in time of peace. More and more children will want to come into our ranks and we must see to it that they may come in their hundreds and their thousands, to learn the tradition of world-wide friendship, to gain the character-training which will help them in their own lives and help in the building of a lasting force of goodwill in the world.

Olave's own feet had indeed been twitching, ever since her arrival in England, to get abroad and to see how her "children" were faring in those European countries which had suffered so devastatingly from the war.

The Guide International Service had been busy all this time preparing for the big work which it did later under the aegis of the Council of British Societies for Relief Overseas. Many books could be written—and at least one has—about the G.I.S. and its activities.

But before the declaration of peace made travel feasible, the World Chief Guide managed somehow to get into France. Accompanied by Mrs Leigh White, Director of the World Guide Association, and by Lady Sandys, she arrived in Dieppe on April 20th 1945, more than a fortnight before V.E. Day. She had been learning French afresh, though she admits that acquiring languages is not one of her talents; but she really needs little beyond her smile to make her audience feel happy and at home.

Scouting and Guiding had been forbidden in France and had gone underground during the years of Occupation, but now the flags were unearthed from their hiding places, and uniforms proudly brought to light, and forty thousand Scouts and Guides came swinging down the Champs Elysées, six abreast, to salute the World Chief Guide. It was a tense moment and filled with emotion for everyone; and the fact that the Movement had not merely survived but had actually increased in numbers and enthusiasm during the years of suppression was a sure proof of B-P's theory that to forbid something to a boy was to arouse his immediate interest in it—whether the thing was cigarettes or Scouting.

It was a busy but most enjoyable visit. Olave talked with General de Gaulle, "a tired man", and with the Archbishop of Paris and, of course, with the Press. She visited the *Centre d'Accueil* at the Gare d'Orsay, where the prisoners of war and tortured *déportés* were arriving back at the rate of ten thousand a day, and where Scouts and Guides were helping with their resettlement.

She addressed three thousand Patrol Leaders—Guides and Scouts together—at the Sorbonne, and found that she had to do without an interpreter and speak entirely in French. They had a riotous evening together.

"Life is pretty full," she wrote, "but how worth while all this is."

After Paris she toured Normandy, visiting the war-ruined cities and villages and finding enthusiasm everywhere in spite of what might have seemed to be unsurmountable difficulties. There was wild excitement among the children and everywhere the warmest of welcomes. Talk, talk, talk, and at Strasbourg her voice gave out and she could only use sign language—but no matter.

The French Commandant sent her in his car over the Rhine, to stand for a few minutes on German soil, while French soldiers played "God save the King". It was only three weeks since Strasbourg had been shelled.

On V.E. Day, when everywhere excitement was at top pitch, Olave crossed into Switzerland and toured through that country, and so on to Rome where, with Mrs Leigh White, she had a private audience with the Pope. Thence to Luxembourg and Belgium, Sweden, Norway and Denmark, cheering and encouraging the newly-emerging Scouts and Guides.

From that hour to this the Chief Guide has travelled almost unceasingly, spending hours of her life in the air. To give in detail the story of her journeyings in any one year would make for repetitive reading and, for those who were not present, a somewhat tedious catalogue. Each visit, though special and precious to her, includes much the same programme of events; the rallies and camp fires for the children; the lunch or tea meetings for their leaders; the reception by Head of State, Lord Mayor, Mayor, or his overseas equivalent; the talks to Press and general public to arouse interest and support; the handing out of awards for good service; the enthusiastic welcomes, the standing ovations, the left handshakes and the regretful farewells.

Yet, for Olave, each visit has its own very special significance; the meetings with old friends and talking with them over earlier days; the revisiting of those many parts of England in which one of her old homes still stands, or with which she had girlhood associations; the records of new enterprises undertaken by Rangers, Guides and Brownies, their rise in numbers and the new heights achieved in carrying out service for the community; the fresh ideas shown in the displays on the rally ground or "stunts" at the camp fire; the new songs to remember and pass on; the new Headquarters building, hut, or camp-ground for her to open. As she looks back on each visit Olave holds in her mind's eye something unique to link her with that particular place, and she never forgets the events or the faces of the people that she met there. In this she is helped too by the numerous cuttings and photographs which reach her afterwards, and which form in her scrapbooks an enduring memento of each separate occasion.

Surely—if one excepts royalty—there was never a more photographed person in the world. If there are ten thousand Scouts at a Jamboree or Guides at a camp, there must be nearly that number of cameras awaiting their opportunity apart from those of the official photographers.

Lists in themselves cannot convey much idea of such happenings, or of the effort involved in carrying out some of the programmes presented; but they do speak of ground covered, so here is a record of places which the Chief Guide visited in 1949, as being typical of so many other years: Bristol, North Surrey, London, Norfolk, Yorkshire, Dorset, Somerset, Essex, Hertfordshire, Hampshire, Wiltshire, Devonshire, West Surrey, Lancashire, Cheshire, Bedfordshire, Middlesex, Cumberland, Westmorland, Northumberland, Durham, Northampton, Staffordshire, Kent; Wales, Ulster, Scotland, Switzerland, Sweden, Norway, Holland, Belgium, Denmark, Egypt, Greece, and the Sudan.

Recalling these visits in her diary Olave writes:

I wonder how many people hear me "talk" in a year, how many letters I write, and how many miles I travel. I certainly have been on the move a good deal and can be thankful that I keep so fit and can go on going on like this, trying to fulfil the task that my Beloved left to me.

Strenuous and exhausting as much of this travel must have been, to Olave it was in every way preferable to Committee work, of which by now she had grown very tired. The drawing up of Constitutions, resolutions, amendments, with lengthy discussions as to their proper wording, was something that she now found very tedious; and she could never quite equate such occasions round the board-room table with the fun and fellowship of Guiding in the field.

July 20th 1943. Meeting at World Bureau of the "Interim Committee". Too much talk and "policy" for me.

Fortunately there were many people willing to relieve her of such
necessary tasks, which she now gladly left to those with more academic
training behind them and the expertise desirable for such work.

At the end of the forties came a much longed-for visit to her beloved
Kenya. "Back home to Nyeri" as she put it and "Oh, how wonderful
to be back".

By the beginning of 1950 she could write: "But now I am not sad,
all the agony having sloughed away in thankfulness for all that we have
had here together."

Olave has revisited her home in Kenya many times and though the
country itself has gone through such drastic changes since the building
of their little house at Nyeri, there are still the unchanging beauties of
nature, the glorious air, the mountain view, and the flowers and birds
which give her fresh joy on each returning visit.

Treetops, in its rebuilt form, is still a pleasure to look forward to and
each time she goes back Olave gives herself the treat of seeing these
many wild animals in their natural habitat.

In 1959 the Queen Mother was paying a visit to Treetops and the
village of Nyeri was *en fête* with thousands of excited Africans lining the
roads in her honour.

It was an anxious time for Sherbrooke Walker because he naturally
wanted Her Majesty to see the wild life at its best, whereas the security
police, necessary on such occasions, proved somewhat of an embarrassment to the animals and the Queen Mother did not see as much as the
normal visitor usually does.

"But her visit has been an enormous success," wrote Olave, "and has
done a lot of good. The Africans have turned up in their thousands and
been captivated by her smile."

While Olave was at Nyeri in 1965, the famous film *Born Free* was in
course of preparation near by, and she described a visit to the two-
legged and four-legged actors in the film.

"Driving out over the plain we came to the ranch where a whole
village has been built, just for the use of the cameramen and actors

and so on. Here are nice little huts for the hundred and thirty Africans and their wives and children, offices for the staff to work in, and large wire cages for the actual performers. Between the times when they are expected to play their parts the lions just lie and sleep, and the surrounding farms supply tons of meat for them. The part of "Elsa" is played, as the film goes on, by seven different lionesses to take the story through several years. First we have the picture of her as a tiny cub with her brother and sister, and then gradually developing into a full-grown lioness. The cubs were lying about, being handled by their girl "keeper" who feeds them with porridge and then has to wipe their faces because they make them so messy!

The film is being made by an American Company and outside the main office at this encampment was a sign post. On one finger it said "Hollywood 10624 miles", and on the other finger, pointing in exactly the opposite direction, was the statement "Hollywood 14802 miles".

Besides meeting the live animal actors I was awfully pleased to meet the leading actress, Virginia McKenna, and still more pleased to know that she had been a Guide. As I went round this wild veldt theatre I met several more of those connected with the whole affair—the young vet. who was there to watch over the animals' health, and to give them tranquillisers as required; the two ladies looking after Virginia McKenna's children; the typist, the secretary, the caterer, the extras and the "pairs of hands"—each and all of them hailed me as a friend with the remark "Oh, yes, I was a Guide in so-and-so Company," or "I started as a Brownie and went up through Guides and Rangers," or "My mother was a Captain and I joined her Guides and then took over the Company later," or "I was a Sea Ranger and it helped me a lot when I went into the WRNS."

This happened to me all the time and it is very stirring to hear that those who had the chance of doing Guiding thoroughly and well have found what they gained of such value to them in their adult life later on.

When, later on, she saw this delightful film in London, it was a happiness to Olave to be able to recognise friends among the two-legged and four-legged performers.

The 1940s had still been years of confusion and bewilderment, when it had been necessary to tread cautiously on unknown or forgotten ways, with rationing still severe and many uncertainties in the air.

With the 1950s came a time of rebuilding, of making up for the years which the war had devoured, of doors opening onto new enterprises and new opportunities, as the nations steadied themselves and counted up their resources for big new efforts.

My journeys have been fairly continuous in 1950 and I can say that never do I visit a town or district without finding some evidence of the infinite value and good that Guiding and/or Scouting is doing for man, woman and child. And hardly does one day pass, even when at home, without my hearing of some incident that bears on the effect of our Movement, whether in retrospect or at the present time. It is thus the cumulative results of our efforts on an astronomical scale that can for ever be our finest stimulant to go on against all odds. We know naturally that our dreams cannot always come true, that hopes may come crashing to the ground and that we are certain to have a proportion of failures and disappointments. These are surely but challenges to our faith and a call to higher endeavour, even if the effect of your service and your example may never be known to you in this life.

At a Training Conference of Guiders in the Western Hemisphere, held in Cuba in 1952, Olave chanced to meet Winston Churchill, who was staying on the island, for the first time in person, though she had always known him as an admirer of her husband's work and a genius at his own. Meeting him unexpectedly in this way, she did not realise that later in the same year she would be dining with his family to celebrate the engagement of his daughter Mary to her own nephew, Christopher Soames, her brother Arthur's son.

She was not able to go to the wedding of this young couple as she was away in the United States doing a strenuous lecture tour.

To rescue her bank balance which, with much travelling, was in rather low water, Olave had undertaken a tour under the Harold Peat agency of New York, in the course of which she visited fifty-seven cities in twenty-five different States and gave a total of a hundred and fifty-eight talks. While combining lectures on Scouting and Guiding with visits to her "children" in all these States she was able at the same time to replenish the emptying coffer.

In a further similar tour the following year she spoke in sixty-one towns in Canada and the United States.

Between times I have gone rushing out to paddle along this lovely beach, all quiet and entirely to myself with nobody except the sea birds. It has been, and is still being, a real breather and though I did a Rally of seventeen hundred yesterday and five hundred last week and have several more functions next week there have been some free days and I have revelled in them. It is all going well and I am very well but putting on weight and my uniform has had to be let out . . .

Eight months non-stop is a bit long when you have quite so tight a schedule as this . . . but it has been fun too with lots of very happi-fying experiences.

CHAPTER XIV

Doors and Other Openings

The lintel low enough to keep out pomp and pride,
The threshold high enough to turn deceit aside,
The doorboard strong enough from robbers to defend,
This door will open at a touch to welcome every friend.

Henry van Dyke

THE Chief Guide loves doors. They shut out the cold, they welcome in friends, they open the way to all adventure and fun.

When, in 1930, the British Guides built their own new Headquarters in Buckingham Palace Road, London, different individuals, groups, counties, and so on, were invited to contribute their special gifts towards the building; two and sixpence for a brick; two pounds ten for a stair; five pounds for a window, and so on. Olave and her husband decided to give a hundred pounds for the entrance doors, through which so many people would come and go in the service of Guiding.

Through a gift from the Guides of Australia thirty years later, known as her "Ice Cream Fund" (each Guide having contributed the cost of an ice-cream when buying one for herself) the Chief Guide has been able to give doors to many Guide buildings throughout the world. She is in constant demand to lay foundation stones and open Guide buildings, and it is to those with which she has had some special connection of this kind that she likes to present a door. So doors will always hold a special significance for her, and her own is certainly an ever-open one to countless friends.

This is doubtless one reason why so many doors are open to her with the "Welcome Mat" always in place.

It has been told in an earlier chapter how Foxlease came into the Guides' possession, and here of course the Chief Guide is always welcome to stay—either to enjoy the quiet beauty of the New Forest or/and—usually and—to talk to some group, training course or Conference, assembled within its doors.

What Foxlease is to the south, Waddow Hall, near Clitheroe, is to northern England, and here too she tries to spend a night or two whenever possible. Towards buying Waddow the Guides of the north themselves raised seven thousand pounds, and Guide gifts have equipped and furnished it.

In Wales there is Broneireon—the generous gift of Lady Davies; and in Northern Ireland there is Lorne, once the stronghold of the Campbells from the Firth of Lorne; while in Scotland Netherurd House, a typically solid Scots mansion, stands among rolling hills twenty-four miles south of Edinburgh. At all these "Guide Houses" in Great Britain there is a warm welcome and a warm bed awaiting the World Chief Guide.

Olave House, too, in London, deserves a special mention, though it comes under a different category. Originally known as "Our Ark", and founded in London in 1939, largely through the efforts of Dame Katharine Furse and Mrs Mark Kerr, this house lived very fully up to its name by giving shelter, in Palace Street, to those many members of the Guide Movement who found themselves stranded in London through one of the many disruptions of war. Later it moved to larger premises in Longridge Road and changed its name to "Olave House". One reason given for this change of name was that the "boyfriend" of the 1960s did not care about dating a girl who came "out of the Ark"; a much more probable reason is that the Guides, recognising how much Olave has done in the establishment of Guide houses round the world, wanted to have one such World House bearing her name.

For a World House it is.

As in Great Britain, each country has its own national Guide Houses for training and central activities, and to be, as the Chief Guide says, "Power Houses" from which the spirit of Guiding flows out into the wider world around. But the World Houses belong equally to every nation.

"Our Chalet" at Adelboden, in Switzerland, was the generous gift of an American, Mrs Storrow. She ("Aunt Helen" to the Baden-Powells) was entertaining them in Bermuda for a short holiday when B-P happened to remark that the Boy Scouts had a Winter Sports Chalet at

Kandersteg, where the Scouts of the nations could meet and make friends while climbing and ski-ing. It would be very nice, he said, if the Guides . . . "But of course," said Mrs Storrow, "they must have one too," and she lost no time in looking for a suitable site, and getting the place built—and paying for it.

Beside "Our Chalet" she built a tiny chalet for herself so that she might be able to go there and watch her gift being used, and nothing could have given her greater joy and pride and satisfaction in her later years than in seeing the gift proving such a success and of infinite value as a meeting place for the Guides and Girl Scouts of all nations.

Mrs Storrow became the first Chairman of the World Association, as well as carrying on her work for the Girl Scouts of America; but her name will always live in Switzerland and in all those countries whose Guides visit "Our Chalet", "Notre Chalet", "Unser Chalet" as it is variously called.

Olave is never happier than when she can seize a few days to spend in this, her Swiss "home". She is usually there for a Conference or other work, but she tries to slip in an extra day or two when possible, for walking, or just gazing:

> For what is life if, full of care,
> We have no time to stand and stare.

For her, and for Guides from any country it is an ever welcoming place.

"Our Cabaña", at Cuernavaca in Mexico, is another World centre, used very largely by Guides in the Western Hemisphere but open to all. "Our Cabana" came into being almost as the result of a chance remark in 1947. Olave was present at a Conference in Cuba and, sitting round the table talking of "Our Chalet", someone remarked that it would be nice to have a chalet at that side of the world—almost as though such a thing could be achieved by the waving of a wand. The more she thought about it, the more the Chief Guide wished it could be done, and while still only a dream the place was jokingly named "Our Cabaña". There was no one person able to present it, so the raising of the necessary funds for such a project was quite a problem. But ten years of hard work and the generosity of hundreds of well-wishers, with faith in the rightness of the cause, brought the place into existence.

At Cuernavaca in Mexico, "Our Cabaña" has wonderful mountain views (many of its visitors had learned of Popacatapetl in their school geography books and were now to see it), and it is a wholly inspiring place filled now with the happy laughter and mixed languages of Guides and Girl Scouts. It is furnished and fitted up in true Mexican style and those who go there for fun or for training, or both, carry home with them, among much else, a knowledge of Mexican history and Mexican crafts.

"Sangam" near Poona in India, is the latest of the World Houses to be opened by the Chief Guide. Its foundation stone was laid in 1964 by Dame Leslie Whateley, then Director of the World Association, and the building was completed three years later. Contributions were made, and funds raised, by many countries, and those British women who had first taken Guiding to India in its earliest days were amongst the first to give their enthusiastic help to the project.

And Olave House is for those who visit England. The latter was officially opened by Olave herself in 1965 and has proved of tremendous value to Guides visiting or working in London—doing for them what its near neighbour Baden-Powell House does for the Scouts. Baden-Powell House is of course another home with a door always open for the Chief Guide.

"Les Courmettes" in France is one of the many national Guide Houses that has delighted to welcome the Chief Guide. It stands on a wide mountain plateau, three thousand feet above the Mediterranean in the south of France. It belongs to the "Federation des Eclaireuses de France" and is a solid stone building with sixteen acres of land surrounding it. Here you see fields divided by stone walls, lavender bushes, sweet-scented broom, the outline of distant hills and, far below, the little inlets of the coast, the islands and the sea. The Chief Guide has stayed there with fifteen hundred enthusiastic Guides who had to bring their camp equipment and themselves up a zig-zag mule track with twenty-nine bends in it—quite a challenge but worth every step.

And so one could go on, enumerating these Guide Houses, but it is enough to say that in every country where Guides exist Olave has her "perch" awaiting her.

It is not only official Guide Houses either that welcome her. In her travels round the world on Guide occasions she has gained an insight into homes of every sort and kind and is equally welcome in all. It may

With Her Majesty
the Queen Mother at
the opening of the
Guide Club, London

With Princess Margaret,
President of the Girl Guides
Association

With Guides in Queensland

Outside Government House, Melbourne

With the Crown Princess
of Japan, 1963

be some small house where her hostess will abandon her own bedroom in order to make her guest comfortable, and where the Chief Guide will make her own bed and help with the washing up—or it may be a stately Government House with two hundred servants and where protocol still holds sway.

Staying with her niece Christian Rawson-Shaw on their farm in Kenya, she writes:

> I have had such a jolly Christmas time with Christian and Clare and the latter's two children up at Songhor. I slept, as before, in the large grass hut which is her guest room—the walls and roof made of thick grass thatch; and my bath water was fetched from the river a mile away by four donkeys carrying petrol tins on their backs, the water supply going on in that somewhat primitive way. They wander along by the hour getting what is needed, and when you have done with the bath water you just throw it out of the door!

Olave loves the primitive life, and the fun of camp, but is equally happy in the statelier houses. She wrote earlier of a visit to the late Princess Royal at Harewood House:

> To stay with the Princess Royal at Harewood. I arrived at 5.45. and she took me for a walk through the gardens and round the lovely lake. Huge ugly house full of treasures. Dined with her and her husband and after dinner sat and talked, she embroidered and I knitted. Most homely.
>
> Breakfasted à trois. Poured with rain so stayed in and typed letters and then H.R.H. took me round the house to see pictures and furniture and her rooms. "Listened in" to the Queen launching the big new ship "Queen Mary", just H.R.H. and me together. Then to Leeds for Rally of about 1,000 Guides and Brownies. I talked and they sang. Then I gave a lecture at the Institute of Science and Art on "Scouting and Guiding and the man who made them". It went well and was an easy topic for me. Lord Harewood took the Chair. Nice warm interested audience. Returned with him to Harewood, supper and bed.

How fortunate it was for Guiding that the Princess Margaret, who from Brownie age (when her sister explained that she had "stout legs for hiking") has always been closely associated with the Movement,

I

was able and willing to succeed the Princess Royal as the beloved President of the Girl Guides Association. By her attendance, not only on special occasions, and at Rallies but also at Council and Committee meetings, her visits and talks with the Chief Guide, Chief Commissioner and others, the Princess has already done more than many Presidents with more time would undertake.

The British Royal Family, in common with the Royal Families of many other countries, have always interested themselves very closely in the work of Scouts and Guides. It was King Edward VII who, in 1910, saw the potentialities of the Movement and suggested to B-P that his work in promoting Scouting was of such importance that it would be worth abandoning his Army career in order to carry it out. Queen Alexandra liked to attend Scout and Guide Rallies, and in their turn King George V and Queen Mary graciously showed their interest and approval, first by the King inspecting a parade of Scouts at Windsor, in the year of his Coronation and, secondly, by their joint encouragement of their family to support the Movement, each Prince in turn playing some part in it.

H.R.H. Princess Mary had attended Guide meetings at her home at Sandringham long before her appointment as President which in 1920 delighted every one. One of her bridesmaids, a Scottish Guide Commissioner, was later to marry the Duke of York and, as Queen, to see her two daughters join up as enthusiastic Guides and Brownies, both in a Buckingham Palace Company and, during the war, at their Windsor home.

It would be impossible to say how much Princess Mary, later the Princess Royal, did for the Guide Movement, not only by her great help in establishing Foxlease as a training centre, which she constantly visited, but also in the encouragement she gave to Guiding everywhere, and perhaps most especially in and around her Yorkshire home. On her visits overseas, too, she always made a point of inspecting the children and meeting and talking with their leaders.

Her sudden death in 1967 deprived the Chief Guide and the whole Movement of a real friend and her loss was deeply mourned.

To return to the subject of "Openings": "I have opened many things in my life," observed the Chief Guide, "but never before have I opened an island."

It was a fine windy day in May 1963.

The little island of Brownsea, off Poole Harbour in Dorset, had been taken over by the National Trust from its owner, Mrs Christie, to be preserved as a site of natural beauty, a bird sanctuary, and a place of pilgrimage for those who appreciated it—among them of course the Scouts and Guides for whom the place especially spells romance.

Brownsea—or Brankeseye in the thirteenth century, from the old English "eig" an island, following the owner's personal name—has even in later years sometimes been known as Branksea. A mile and a half long by three-quarters of a mile wide, it has an area of five hundred acres. Its sides are covered with fir groves while the interior is broken up into miniature glens and hills, rising in places to a height of ninety feet, where heaths and wild flowers grow in profusion.

The Castle, built in the reign of Henry VIII and strengthened in the time of Charles I, was an important defence of Poole. Being at the mouth of the harbour it commanded all shipping passing in and out. Smugglers must have disliked it very much. It is recorded that in 1581 a complaint was lodged that

> The Goovner of Bronkseye doth molest the inhabitants of the towne and will not suffer them to pass any persons from Northaven Point, but doth threaten them to shoote at them and violently doth take their money from them which is not only a great hindrance to poor men that were woonte to gayne that wayse but also an infrynginge of our liberties wherefore we think it very necessary to be remedyd.

Nothing, however, seems to have resulted from this protest for it appears that later this "Goovner" added deeds to his threats and shot at a vessel *The Bountiful Gifte*, killing its owner and captain.

Brownsea was at one time attached to the Abbey of Cerne in Dorset and was the site of a hermit's cell. During the Civil War the Castle was held by a Parliament garrison.

Later it became a private dwelling house and various additions were made from time to time.

Colonel Waugh came into possession of the island in 1848 and spent large sums in its development, building some cottages and the beautiful little church of St Mary the Virgin.

In 1896 the Castle was burnt down and rebuilt and the van Raalte family bought it in 1901. Charles van Raalte, the wealthy stockbroker son of a Dutch immigrant, had the idea of importing and raising bulbs there.

At a houseparty in Ireland he and his wife met, and made friends with, Baden-Powell, with the result that in 1907 B-P "borrowed" the Island from them as a suitable place to try out in freedom and seclusion his new idea of Scouting for Boys.

From that little camp of a few boys under his personal direction has sprung the world-wide Scout and Guide movement; so it was only appropriate that when the National Trust took over the island they should invite Olave Lady Baden-Powell to perform the opening ceremony. There, in 1932, B-P had received the Freedom of Poole, in recognition of his services to the youth of the world; and there, in 1950, Olave herself had been made a Freeman.

Strangely enough Olave had spent the last four years before her marriage at Parkstone near by, and had sailed with her friends round the island, little dreaming of what, in after years, would be her connection with the place. During her engagement in 1912 she had walked there with B-P—now, here she was again, in a place filled with memories.

The little island church of St Mary the Virgin, unused for years, was this day reopened and rehallowed by the Archdeacon of Dorset, with the clergy and choir of St Peter's Church, Parkstone—the church in which in 1912 Olave had been married. The wedding had been a very quiet one without guests, but one person who had been present at it—the verger— was also present at this church rehallowing, after more than fifty years.

More recently the parish of St Peter's, Parkstone, has maintained the link with the Baden-Powell family by presenting a memorial pew to another St Peter's—the little church at Nyeri in Kenya, near to which is the Founder's grave.

To open an island does not fall to the lot of very many people and Olave certainly enjoyed her day there which, beginning with lunch at the Yacht Club, Sandbanks, included a visit to her old home at Grey Rigg, Lilliput and ended with a Rally of Dorset Guides.

The problem of social integration between the immigrant population and the dwellers in the large cities of Britain might almost have been at the back of B-P's mind when he drew up his schemes for Brownies and Cubs as junior branches of the big Movement that he had designed. Yet in those days no-one could ever have imagined an invasion from over-seas such as has occurred in the last two decades.

But "Be Prepared" not only for what is probable but also for what is possible, was one of his key mottoes. And the very elastic framework of Scouting and Guiding was so designed that it had no sort of problem in opening its doors to the children of other races and nationalities when they arrived with their parents in Great Britain.

Hundreds of immigrants in the big cities begin their social integration as members of Troops and Companies and perhaps more especially Cub and Brownie Packs, where they find friends ready-made, anxious to greet them with the well-known signs and salutes, the universal Laws and Promises, and the games and fun that belong to Guiding and Scouting wherever they may be. It is one activity in which the races here can all meet and mix with harmony of thought, and the World Chief Guide has had a wide experience of such meeting and mixing and its results, in many a country in the course of her travels. This has been confirmed by leaders who have welcomed the little strangers and made them at home in their midst.

"These West Indian children are terrific runners," commented a Brownie leader in North London. "They win most of the games but their friends don't mind because they can usually beat them in other fields."

"We have no prejudice on either side, either from children or parents," says another Guider. "Our immigrants are rather boisterous and love to chat, so they need perhaps a little extra attention at first, but I've seen a tremendous improvement in their English and in their understanding of our ways through this mix-up."

These Packs and Companies, like many others throughout the country, have long waiting-lists, with not enough leaders to go round.

"Who are you?" asked the Chief Guide of a little group of children of Brownie age but not wearing uniform.

"We're the waiting-list," replied the leader of this eager little gang!

Nevertheless, membership does expand year by year, and in 1969 the number of Guides in Britain increased by twenty thousand.

The Movement is certainly helping to build up trust for the future among peoples who really long for man-made barriers to be removed. In an age of permissiveness and general lowering of morals, the Guide creed of hopefulness, happiness, and helpfulness to all is one of the really constructive things in a difficult world.

It was with great delight that early in 1959 the Chief Guide heard that the Salvation Army "Life Guards" had thrown in their lot with Guiding, and added their own ten thousand members to the Guide ranks.

This is something that I have longed for for years and years. As I write I can look back on an occasion that happened during my earliest days in Guiding. There had been a very jolly Rally with displays by every Company, and, to end up with, a huge camp fire. As I walked round to talk with each group of Guides I came upon a little party of girls in grey, sitting right away from the fire but gazing with longing towards it. I did not then know who they were or why they were not with us, so I asked and one of them said—"Well, we don't really belong; we do all the same sort of things as the Guides but we are not Guides so we can't come to the Camp Fire." That is the first picture that comes to my mind's eye of my contact with the Guards; but now and again, through the years, I have seen them about their lawful occasions, having their own meetings and no doubt carrying on their work with just the same eager good spirit that is shown by Guides. I felt so sad that they were not quite "with us", especially as their brothers, the Salvation Army Scouts, were all a part of the great Scout Movement. Then, when I went to Canada some years ago, I met a big bunch of Salvation Army Guides and discovered that there they had linked up and were wearing our Guide blue with their Salvation Army badges, showing that they were in *two* good things. And so now, here in Britain, two good things are joining up together to make one bigger good thing, and with more to give than either had before. For unity is strength.

CHAPTER XV

Perpetual Motion

Through all the travels of our lady Chief when she makes ceaseless and uncomfortable journeys to give her reviving message of encouragement to Guides and their hard-pressed leaders near and far, may she be strengthened, and everyone who comes into contact with her be re-inspired by the Founder's vision for the youth of the world.

A Guide's Prayer

TWICE in the 1930s Olave had toured Australasia with the Chief Scout; since then she has toured it again three times—in the forties, the fifties, and the sixties, and her friends in that continent are so many that to her each visit seems like coming home.

Over ten thousand miles in 57 hours! It sounds fantastic, doesn't it, but it is true because I have just done it. Here I am in Australia on Tuesday October 22nd and only last Saturday night, having done my packing and got all my letters written and my desk cleared and my home ready to be put to bed for the winter, I took off from London and flew in stages over bits of fourteen countries. France and Switzerland first, and after about five hours we dropped down and I walked about for half an hour or so at Athens while we re-fuelled. Then we skipped over Turkey, Iraq and Saudi-Arabia and, landing for another hour, I did walk on Pakistan soil in the middle of the night. In the dark we hopped across India to Calcutta and passing over Burma I paid my first call on Thailand. Leaving Siam behind we skipped across the sea to Malaya and there a surprise was in store for me as we landed—two hours late—at Singapore at the tippy end of the long strip which has now become the Federation of Malaya. A grand little Guard of Honour of Guiders and Rangers turned out to greet me and we just had time for a little party, hand-shakings and talking and laughing together, the cutting of a grand cake made in the shape of a trefoil, and a bit of a sing-song, before taking off again in the darkness at ten o'clock.

But that wasn't all, by any means, for that night. Landing at Djakarta, the capital of Indonesia, there they were again—not quite so many as the Movement there is young and small, but they were full of eagerness and gave me a most thrilling welcome at a midnight Rally. The leaders had arranged a charming programme and had even put on a most attractive display of dancing; and then we sang the World Guide song, and—though English, or should I say Scottish, is not exactly their language—we all held hands in a large circle and ended up with "Auld Lang Syne". You would hardly have expected that to happen in Indonesia, but this Guiding does make for surprise happenings . . .

In the United States and in Canada too Olave has close friends in every state and every province, and loves to spend the winter months on that side of the Atlantic. She loves the speed of flight, no less than the speed of a friend's car racing her across Canada or round the United States.

In 1959 she visited fourteen Central and South American countries and this journey had to be done in the spring and summer months which she usually loves to spend in England. This must have been one of the most physically exhausting tours, as the Guiders and Guides with whom she came in contact were for the most part Spanish and Portuguese speaking people, hospitable, keen and eager to have her among them and to talk to her, but unable to speak English. To talk in the free and easy manner which is natural to her, but with an interpreter always at her elbow, has its difficulties for the Chief Guide, but she manages somehow to surmount them and to add numbers of new friends to her collection.

This journey began in Brazil:

It is a miracle this flying. Leaving home on the afternoon of Saturday, I was here in Recife in time to go to church on Whitsunday morning, a charming little English church set among palm trees and scarlet hibiscus and with electric fans blowing to keep us cool. The organ had been given as a memorial to the British who went from this country to die in the war, and besides putting a brass plaque to record their names a fund was raised to give the organ and an electric blower for it and to keep it in repair—such a thoughtful wise gift.

From Brazil—after ten days in that country—to Uruguay for a few days visit and then to Argentina for a week before flying over the Andes to Chile.

The wife of the British Ambassador to Chile had been first a Guider in Canada and then in Germany and then in London, and there she was in uniform, cheering on the group of Guides and Brownies of the British community which had only just been started, in time to join in with the Chilean Guides camp fire and to add their contribution by singing "Who are these, swinging along the road?"—which I don't suppose had ever before been sung on this side of the Andes.

And so on to Peru where, at 10.30 at night at Lima there were about four hundred Guides and Rangers, Cubs and Scouts waiting for her at the airport.

Here is the son of our former County Commissioner in Surrey and one Queen's Guide I had seen at the Windsor camp. One Scouter I had met at two Jamborees and one man had—as a Cub—sung to me at the huge Rally in Paris in 1945. A Guider from the Congo had seen me there in 1950 and again in Belgium last summer . . . While walking on to a school ground for a rally here in Lima, an oldish man greets me and tells me that he was the founder of one of the first Scout troops in Birkenhead in 1910; another friendly person who rushed to shake my hand had been a Guider in Sussex when I was County Commissioner there in 1916—and here we all are, meeting again in Peru. The wife of Her Majesty's Ambassador here had been a Guide in Paris and in England and told me how much it had meant to her when arriving in a new country to find herself welcomed immediately by Guides.

And so it went on. In every one of these countries there were old friends, as well as the new ones, to be greeted. Ecuador:

There was a bit of a revolution a few days before I got here and unfortunately 500 people were killed in the streets; and as everyone was busy settling down my visit was a bit quieter than in some of the

other countries . . . Panama hats are not made in Panama but in
Ecuador; and the kapok in your cushions and pillows is probably
made from Ecuador's giant ceiba trees, while many of our modern
aeroplanes are made from Ecuadorian balsa—that lightest of all woods
that made the Kontiki raft.

I was given the Freedom of the City of Guayaquil by the Mayor
which made us feel very proud and grand as the Guides had never
before had so much official notice taken of them.

Thence to Colombia and Panama—where she was presented with a
Master Key to the Canal—Costa Rica, Nicaragua, Salvador. To
commemorate her visit to El Salvador the President offered a Scholarship to be given in perpetuity for a Guider or Guide to go and be
trained for a month each year in some other country—to be known as the
OLAVE BADEN-POWELL SCHOLARSHIP.

This plan will be most valuable not only in giving a Guide or Guider
the wonderful experience of meeting and mixing with members of the
Movement in another country, but also in enabling her to take to
them news and methods from El Salvador and to bring back news and
ideas from other places—a two-way traffic. And I think that is a very
valuable thing for us all to remember. When you go to a camp, a
rally, or a meeting in another place you are leaving something behind
you as well as carrying something away with you—and we must be
careful that what we leave behind will be something happy, useful,
and good.

So on to Guatemala—that freedom-loving country where on their
coat of arms they have a quetzal, a very rare bird of brilliant plumage
which values its freedom so much that it dies in captivity. It is their
symbol.

One of the most interesting things that I came across here was a big
school run by an order of nuns—the St Mary Knoll. These fine
women go off to various parts of the world to take Christianity and
Education and, unlike other nuns that I have come across, they
were not wearing habits but were in Guide uniform and obviously
felt that a knowledge of Guiding and Scouting is a form of equipment
for a teacher.

After Guatemala there were two days under the British flag in Honduras, and then on to Mexico, and to "Our Cabaña" which it is always a great joy to Olave to visit.

Cuernavaca, near to which town "Our Cabaña" is to be found, was the home of Cortez, when he claimed Mexico for Spain in the sixteenth century.

"Our Cabaña" has dormitories for about fifty girls and here the Chief Guide meets Spanish-speaking Guides from Peru and Chile; Portuguese-speaking Guides from Brazil; English-speaking Guides from Canada and the Caribbean; French-speaking Guides from Canada and Haiti; Dutch from Aruba and Curacao and Girl Scouts from the U.S.A. A medley of tongues all speaking the same language—the language of Guiding!

In all these countries the Chief Guide was delighted to find enthusiasm growing for the Guide training, though in some places their only literature on the subject was in English. On her return to England she was able, through her Australian "Ice Cream Fund" to send parcels of literature in their own language to help them.

There are always some amusing incidents to recall from these flying visits.

On arriving in one town I met the local Guide President, who told me that her own daughter would be at the Rally—among the thousands of others—that evening. I said "Tell her to stop me during the inspection and say which she is". And as I was walking along the rows of smart happy-looking Guides a little voice piped up, loud and clear, "I am my mother's daughter!"

The Guide International Commissioner for Chile, who had been an invaluable interpreter at all the various functions in Santiago, later wrote this charming tribute to the British generally and to the Chief Guide in particular:

I know you believe all people to be alike, and that you live for this maxim. You will therefore shake your head in disapproval if I tell you that because you are British all over you are so brave and enterprising. Was there a war and was there misery? So what! Was there hunger, ration cards and belt tightening after the war? Well, what if there was. Did they suffer cold, disease and poverty? What of it?

And so it is with you. Is there a job to be done? Yes, there is, so I'm never tired! Do people want to see me? Yes they do and I must let them. Could I give yet another speech, open another meeting, please another host by being present at his reception? Well, if there is I must be there because I must not disappoint them.

And if the Guiding principles you so wisely outlined during your numerous meetings are to mean a way of living, healthy, joyful and useful too, *you* yourself will always count as an outstanding example of selflessness, duty, and overcoming small and sometimes big difficulties. I personally thank you for having allowed me to share your way of life if only for a few days, because your example will inspire me for a life-time.

"Did you have a nice holiday?" friends will sometimes ask Lady Baden-Powell, when she returns from a long tour like that.

"Holiday—my foot," she might well reply.

Much as she enjoys the contacts made in every part of the world that she visits, there is not as a rule very much "holiday" about the Chief Guide's outings. Everything is planned, down to the last detail, by the "host" country, and every minute of her available time is filled in with busy activities for her as well as for those that she visits.

And the best-laid plans do sometimes break down and, added to the ordinary exertions of catching planes at daybreak and so on, there are the additional worries when, usually through nobody's fault, the planes do not fly.

Before the Chief Guide started on this long and exacting and hurried tour, looking in on all these fourteen countries for a few days of hard work in each, it had been suggested that, as planes were so often delayed, it would be as well not to have Guides awaiting her arrival at airports.

This was ignored, and there they were—bless them—in rows, awaiting me with such kindly friendly open arms—all mixed in with Press photographers who swarm round snapping their nasty little flash bulbs at me and doubtless getting some truly dreadful pictures—as well as some good ones—of the Guides and me.

Air travel holds no terrors for the Chief Guide, and she loves its speed and efficiency.

Air hostesses, too, are a specially fine lot of young women, and one does so admire their courtesy, efficiency, quiet manners, friendly smiles—always ready to comfort people who feel ill—and ready for any emergency. (One had an accouchement to deal with not long ago.)

But circumstances can certainly let you down on occasion. As she wrote in November 1956:

This travelling isn't always either easy or fun, and it can be wearing and worrying on occasion. Malta was delightful and all went well there, meetings, parties with Guiders, a Rally of Scouts, Cubs, Guides and Brownies, and as it rained we had to hold it in the Scouts' hall, into which we were squeezed like sardines—but happy sardines . . . And then, when the news was so bad (Suez), I was told that I might not get on even to Khartoum. I thought I had better get across the Mediterranean, towards my objectives, and with constant tele-phonings, and people saying first that I couldn't go and then that I could, I went hopefully to the Airport. A plane came in an hour late and I flew in it to Tripoli—a place I had never expected to visit— getting there at near midnight. Long delay on arrival as I had then and there to get my passport visa-d to allow me to go to the hotel in the town—of course with no bed booked so I didn't know where I might sleep. However I got into the town eventually, found a Hotel, and went to bed, wondering where and what would be the next move in the game. The BOAC office said I had better come and see them, so I took a carriage with a nice horse and found that they thought I might get on to Khartoum-bound plane that evening, so I went back to the Hotel and waited. An hour later a telephone to say there was no seat on the plane. Two hours later the Manager rang up to say he would himself take me to the Airport (20 miles away) and we might manage a chance seat. 6 p.m. got to Airport, sat, walked about, sat again, and in came a plane. No luck, quite full. Fortunately there was a res- taurant, so one could get food; so hopefully I sat and waited for a seat. Full—quite full—but a third plane would be in "soon", so again I sat waiting. "Soon" was 3.30 a.m. Again no luck, so back again I went to bed at 4.30 at Tripoli still when I ought to have been a thousand miles south of it. Sent frenzied telegram to Khartoum regretting non-arrival and in real agitation as to when I could get there. Then the Manager had a bright idea and said he could get me back across the Mediterranean in an Italian plane and I might be able to get a plane in Rome. So after another twenty-four hours wait I got a plane and landed in Sicily, with endless bother over another flight ticket and payment of another twenty-two pounds for the Italian plane. Arrived at Catania, the Rome-bound plane was full, but after four hours wait there was another and I at last reached Rome at 11 p.m. No Hotel booked of course but I found one and slept back in Europe again. Sunday morning, rang up BOAC and they thought they might get me on to a plane but uncertain, and had I got a visa for Sudan? I had not thought of such a thing as I was to be a guest of the Sudan Government. But they would not give me a seat without one so I tore round to the Sudan Passport Office and then— wonder of wonders—the BOAC had got word from London and there would be a seat for me on their plane that afternoon. Much relieved I got to their office at 3.30 and waited as usual, proving the saying that in air travel you wait to rush then rush to wait. At last at 7 p.m. we boarded the aircraft, taxi-d to the runway, and then turned back as there was "something a little wrong". After another four hours we boarded it again and how thankful I was to settle down to—did you say sleep? Not much, but how blessed it was to feel, with the droning of the engines through the night, that I was going south at last on this important lap of my trip. With dawn over the desert came breakfast, beautifully served by the Air Hostess and steward, and as the sun blazed in the sky there was the Nile and Khartoum and across the River Omdurman, the huge sprawling Arab town of white houses looking like square boxes. The Guide people had met every plane at the Airport for two days expecting me any minute, and so now had given me up as hopeless. So when I rang up I asked whether, having dished their four days programme made jointly with the Scouts, by failing to arrive. I should go straight on to Uganda instead. But they said STOP, we do want you. So then, in spite of all the alterations and cancellations of the former plans I spent a great day with them there. Quickly the telephones buzzed and in that short fourteen hours

I was received by the President of the Republic, who was most kind and interested in Scouts and Guides. It was delightful visiting him in the fine big Palace where I had had a Guide Rally in 1949. I was also received by the Prime Minister who had himself been a Scout and is therefore specially interested. Lunch party with Guiders and Committee members; tea party in their excellent Headquarters which I had opened in 1949; large dinner party for about 50 interested men and women, the Ministers for Education, Cultural Development, and so on. And I also called on the Mahdi.

In darkness at 4 a.m. next morning I was in the air again, speeding south in a beautiful Ajax filled with sleeping men, women, children and babies, who had come through the night all the way from London. Now I had caught up with my schedule, and the rose pink dawn over the desert seemed like an omen for the rest of my tour even though the news that filtered through from people and radio spoke of terrible happenings in Hungary and elsewhere, and the cruel unhappiness being created again in our world. We in Scouting and Guiding must do our utmost in thought and prayer and effort to counter this, and to spread goodness ever more widely—with sympathy for these sufferings . . . And here I am in Uganda at last.

No, travelling on those fixed schedules is not all easy and carefree by any means. As anyone who works with children, even in a small way, knows, you must not let them down and if you have undertaken to be there you must try by hook or crook to fulfil your promise to them. In some of these journeys the Scouts and Guides have travelled hundreds of miles by road or train—with money saved up for the outing—just to have a little meeting with their Chief, and it is a terrible worry to her if she has to disappoint them.

Occasionally, too, their own arrangements break down through no fault of their own. As in Canada in 1961:

One little band of Eskimos came from Labrador to St John's by boat for five hours, and then they flew for the first time in their lives. They had never left home before and it was an adventure for them seeing a big town for the first time. They had saved up for months of course for the long trip and one girl had got her First-class Badge. And then, owing to weather conditions, the plane could not take them back, so they had to return by land and sea and to leave St John's before the big Rally which was so disappointing for them.

This long tour, planned to take the Chief Guide first to the U.S.A., then right across Canada and round the U.S.A. again, was one of the very few occasions when she herself has been the cause of cancellations.

After a successful time in Halifax, Lunenberg, Moncton, St John's, New Brunswick, and Fredericton, she arrived at Charlottetown, Prince Edward Island, and at a Guiders' lunch party had a sudden fainting attack and was hurried away to hospital. Much to her chagrin the Canadian authorities decided to cancel the remainder of the tour—no doubt quite rightly—but though a compulsory three weeks' rest in hospital was probably the best thing that could happen, the thought of the disappointment and upset that she was causing was very grievous to Olave, and she would willingly have risked a second heart attack rather than let everyone down in this way. But Miss Henrietta Osler, Chief Commissioner for Canada, was adamant. *They* were not going to allow their Chief Guide to kill herself, however much she wanted to—she was much too valuable—and poor Olave was forced to accept her fate. Disguised as "Mrs Brown" (for the tour being cancelled she could not now appear in uniform anywhere in Canada) she drove with Mrs Pepler and Mr and Mrs Nevill back into the States for a recuperative holiday. "I do feel so thwarted and silly," she wrote home, "not being able to make any contacts at all . . . I ought to be thankful for this holiday and I try to think I am."

On December 23rd she got back into uniform for the first time for two months, and by February was once more in full swing, carrying out her usual round of daily engagements in spite of having been advised to take it easy. "Taking it easy" is not one of her favourite occupations.

A shortened tour across Canada had been rearranged, so she was able to compensate in some way for the disappointment caused.

Olave's only other illness during these many years of travel, necessitating an operation for the removal of gall stones, happened during the Christmas holiday which had been planned to divide into two stages a long tour in Australia; and she was thereafter able to carry out her full programme.

With Scouts in Jamaica, 1964

A wonderful smile from a Brownie in Canada

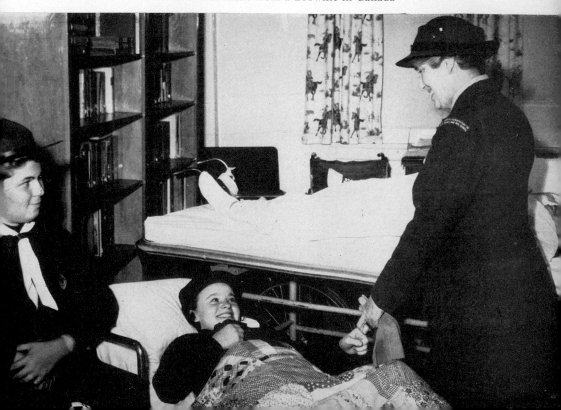

With the author at the Johnston Historical Museum, Brunswick, U.S.A.

With Duke of Edinburgh Award winners outside Buckingham Palace

There have been no interruptions to her constant travels since those two episodes, but the Chief Guide does now make a few concessions to her advancing years.

"I have begun a new phase and have got a new phrase," she said in 1969, having reached the age of eighty, "I am now in my semi-retirement."

Semi-retirement, one supposes, means different things to different people. For Olave, in addition to her normal home visits, it meant journeys to Kenya, Uganda, Finland (two visits for Scout and Guide World Conferences), Nigeria (for Jubilee Guide camps, determinedly held in a war-stricken country), Canada, the United States (for a big National Jamboree) the Channel Islands, Switzerland, and Belgium, with long and exacting programmes in each place. In Brussels, where the Guides were carrying out a rather unusual Good Turn of counting sea-gulls for their country's Natural History Department, she was received by Queen Fabiola and spent an interesting hour with her Majesty discussing the Guide Movement.

Amongst the many busy hours of this first year of "semi-retirement" Olave did, however, manage to seize two lovely days in September to visit her beloved old home village of Bentley and to renew her acquaintance with Hampshire's lanes and hedges while picking pounds of blackberries.

Her old home, Pax Hill, was not relinquished by the War Department until long after Olave was established in her Grace and Favour apartment at Hampton Court. What then was to happen to Pax Hill? She handed it over to Guide Headquarters and for a few years it served as a Homecraft Training School for Guides, who received there an excellent course in all domestic subjects under expert tuition; but it was found that the limited accommodation there did not allow such a scheme to pay its way, and eventually the house was sold.

Pax Hill is now carrying on good work as a school, but there is always the hope that a house which holds so much of the history of Scouting and Guiding may one day come back into the hands of one or other of these bodies—or perhaps of both—as a Museum or place of pilgrimage.

The village too holds so much B-P history, with its War Memorial Hall, whose architect he was; its prominent Village Sign, the "Open Book" which he designed; and its "B-P Fishing Association".

K

In the church which they attended when at home, and in which both their daughters were married, the Scouts of Hampshire have placed a table commemorating his life and great interest in the welfare of Bentley parish and village.

CHAPTER XVI

Centenary

JULY 1957, and the whole of England seemed to be ablaze with flowers.
For miles round Sutton Coldfield, in lovely leafy Warwickshire, all the
flower beds, whether in municipal parks, roundabouts, town or country
gardens, had been planted with Scout badges and emblems, the initials
B-P and the dates 1857-1957 predominating, in every conceivable
form of floral art—leaving passers-by in no sort of doubt about what
was being celebrated.

This of course was the centenary of the birth of Baden-Powell, and
it happened also to be the Golden Jubilee of the Boy Scout Movement,
which he had founded at the age of fifty; so the Scouts had a two-fold
reason for their World Jamboree being held in the middle of England.

The Guides, for their part, were holding four Centenary camps—in
Canada, in the Philippines, in Switzerland, and in England—this latter
taking place in Windsor Great Park, graciously lent for the purpose by
Her Majesty the Queen.

Other countries, too, were celebrating the event. In South Africa, for
example, thousands of trees the names of which began with the letter
"B" or "P" were being planted, the Guides undertaking their care
until they reached maturity.

In India special "centenary" efforts were being made by Guides and
Brownies in the growing of food, and in campaigns for literacy among
the backward people.

Preparations for these and many other special events in the parent
country were well in hand when Olave returned from Africa, where she
had been visiting Guides in many places scattered across Northern and
Southern Rhodesia—tiny happenings when contrasted with those that
were to come, but equally important in her eyes.

We have tiny Rallies at each stopping place—with usually two or
perhaps three Companies, and perhaps one or two Brownie Packs.

Very few are able to afford any uniform, other than a tie—to pin their badge on—and as these people never wear hats they just have a head-band of yellow, blue, or red, as a Company colour.

These little Companies are usually attached to Mission Schools, and the children base many of their "displays" on stories from the Gospels. Though they have little enough in the way of dressing-up materials, Africans, wherever they may be, have a very keen sense of drama and invariably succeed in getting their story across, with something of its spirit as well.

In the course of her tour the Chief Guide was treated to several presentations of the Parable of the Good Samaritan, each one different from the last, but in every case each part of the story was most vividly demonstrated, even to the extent of doing real "first-aid" on the wounded man and then lifting "him" carefully and correctly on to a donkey (Guides covered with a brown blanket) to carry him away to the inn.

These Guides gave me a delightful welcome. Their singing is quite lovely, and yet they know not a note of actual "music" but sing naturally in harmony. They invent words to the songs as they go along. They have some lovely dances of their own and do them with such verve and gaiety. At one village they had learned an old English country dance "Galopede"—and I think some of the Guides at home would have laughed to see me joining in, on a wide dusty ground, in grilling sun, all of us cavorting around together with large grins on our faces.

(And this was the person who, in 1942, had described herself as a "doddery old bird"!)

Olave's next assignment, during that busy year was in Ghana (formerly the Gold Coast) a place so well known to B-P in his soldiering days and now to have its independence.

Scouts and Guides were having their share in all the Independence celebrations and, as well as being present as an official guest, Olave was able to see something of their progress and activities during this visit.

A significant fact about these newly emerging independent countries is that, while they wish to throw off many so-called "western" ideas, they all want to keep their Scouts and Guides, and for this we must give some credit to the wide-minded men and women who took the Movement to them in earlier days.

The African head of the Guides in newly independent Uganda wrote:

Your tour has been a sign of love, encouragement and appreciation and we really hope there will be good results and progress everywhere in Uganda. We have a very important task on our hands especially at this juncture when most European ladies who have rendered excellent service for the Movement are leaving shortly for good, and others have already left the country; hence it is now up to us to take over straightway, without delay, with enthusiasm, determination, co-operation, and above all with *love*. It would be a great pity for our now independent country if Guiding faded away as it is of so great benefit to our daughters and to the well-being of the country as a whole.

The Centenary celebrations in England opened with a great Thanksgiving service in Westminster Abbey on February 22nd, and the Chief Guide was home in time to join in this, and to receive the thousands of greetings which came to her from all parts of the world.

The Jamboree, Rallies, and Camps of that year were something very special and very spectacular, and were attended by the Queen and the Duke of Edinburgh, other members of the Royal Family, the Prime Minister, and many other invited guests, besides vast crowds of the general public, mingling with the Scouts and Guides.

The Chief Guide took part in as many of these events as could be fitted in, and spent much time on the road between Sutton Park and Windsor Park. To open the World Camp at Windsor, thence to the Jamboree at Sutton Park for some days, back for the closing scenes of Windsor camp and then north again to "close" the Jamboree were just a few of her engagements in July and August. All these events were world news and she was indispensable at them all. It was a time for her of poignant memories as well as of joy and thanksgiving, and she was in everyday demand for speeches, messages, Press, television and radio interviews.

Her closing remarks on the last night at Windsor were carried—

together with specially worked "samplers" depicting Windsor Castle—
to every part of the world where Guides existed.

You have camped for this wonderful week beneath the shadow of a
great old fortified Castle—and as you go out from this place to take
up your normal work in the world outside, each one of you will carry
with you in your mind's eye a picture of this ancient home of Kings
and Queens, with its walls and towers built strong and secure to
withstand enemy invaders.

This Castle is a Queen's home, but remember, all of you, that each
one of us—whether we live in a castle, a cottage, a cabin or even a
tent—has within herself fortifications strong to resist evil, to keep out
the invading enemies of fear and distrust, to overcome what is bad and
to strengthen and develop what is good. It is no use shutting out evil
unless we put goodness and happiness in its place and that is where
we, in our Movement, are so fortunate.

It would be foolish to shut our eyes to the fact that there is much in
the world that is wrong and weak and unhappy. Our Founder told us
to "see the worst but look at the best" and as guides you have each
one of you within your castle a strong fortification of happiness, of
friendly goodwill and the spirit of service to all around.

Remember it is not what you have, but what you give that brings
happiness. That is why, as members of our great Movement, it is so
important for each one of you to try your hardest to become skilful
and clever with your hands, alert and ready in your minds, and great
of heart, so that by these means you may bring friendship and happiness to others and thereby gain it for yourselves.

We take in in order that we may give out.

Every one of us who has camped here this week has gained something and most of us have gained a great deal. We have imbibed fresh
stores of health and happiness and good fellowship in order that,
as we return to everyday life outside the camp, we may have these
things in ever fuller measure to hand out to our homes, to our companies, to our countries and to all around us whoever and wherever
we may be.

So when you see in your mind's eye, as you will for years to come,
this old Castle and this lovely Centenary Camp in which we have all

shared, let it be a reminder to each one of you, not only of the Promise and Law of our sisterhood, but also of that spirit of world friendship and world fellowship which alone can bring about God's Kingdom of peace and goodwill for which we so often pray. God bless you all.

It was a moving moment, and, as darkness fell on the camp fire circle, the lights of thousands of torches suddenly shone out on the departing figures of the Princess Royal and the Chief Guide, giving a splendour and radiance which seemed to come straight from the heart of every Guide as she held her light aloft.

A young Norwegian girl's letter was typical of many:

My year's stay in England started with the Guides' world camp at Windsor; dusky summer evenings at the camp fire when each country gave us something of its very self; daily work in our group where friendship was made over a difficult task; eager asking and answering, to learn as much as possible about Guiding everywhere; your visits to the camp when at last we saw our Chief of whom we had read and heard so much; all these happy memories on which we can live for a long time . . . I shall try to bring back to my Guides at home some of the riches I have gained and the friendship and happiness I have met.

*   *   *

"Every Adventure must have a beginning; but it is in the continuing of it until it is thoroughly finished that yields the true glory."

Olave had been made an honorary member of the 1st Gilwell Park Troop—a coveted honour to be won normally by those Scouters who had gone through a very tough course of training, entitling them—if they succeeded—to wear the Gilwell scarf and the "beads on a bootlace" devised by B-P to be a sign that the wearer had the roots of the matter in him.

In her travels throughout the world it was always an intense pleasure to the Chief Guide to meet a wearer of this insignia in some out of the way place and to talk of Gilwell; and now she was to be given this even closer link with the place from which the Founder had taken his title and with which he had been so closely associated.

On her marriage in 1912 Olave had "adopted" the Scouts, had worked as a lady Scoutmaster, and worn their uniform, long before she had been drawn into Guiding; so it seemed fitting that now, in her new capacity, she should be invited to address this unique body as they assembled at Gilwell for their Reunion in the B-P Centenary year.

Beginning with Drake's statement, quoted above, she went on to give to a new generation a reminder of the meaning and methods of Scouting as laid down by the Founder.

This philosophy of an old sea dog would seem an apt text for you, the Scouters of today who continue the Founder's work, and a reminder of the glory that may be yours.

Scouting had its beginning in days which—to those of us who can look back fifty years—seem to have been very much simpler. Yet to the pioneers of Scouting in those days—with no training to guide them—it must have been an uphill job to get the Movement on to its feet. All honour to them.

It is for you who continue their work to see that in these ever more complicated days we preserve the true essence of Scouting in all its simplicity, its purity and its entirety. With all the extra scientific knowledge of today, all the modern gadgets and processes and the mechanical aids to easy living, let us never forget that Scouting is a method of character training.

None of the ingredients which the Founder put into his Movement were actually new. Most of them had been known to adventurers down the ages. Knotting and splicing must have been practised by the old sea rovers long before he taught his Africans in Ashanti to tie reliable knots for the bridges that they had to make. Tracking, observation, deduction, had long been practised by pioneers and explorers, as knowledge of first-aid had been the handmaid of missionaries.

No, the adventure then was in the mixture; the discovery of how to develop body, mind and spirit in such a way that the boy had a chance to grow into a balanced citizen and to be the man that God intended him to be—happy, healthy, handy and helpful.

We all know of other youth Movements—horrid term—in which one or two aspects of character training—excellent in themselves—

tend to outweigh the others and to make the finished article un-
balanced. We look regretfully at those which are so engaged in toughening the body that they neglect the mind: more critically still at those
which allow no opportunity for spiritual training as well as those
which deliberately flout it.

The genius of our Founder lay not in inventing anything new but
in combining those ingredients which go to form character in such
proportion that, while making a dish palatable to every normal boy,
he offered something that would build him up in every direction.

And that is where you come in because through your Gilwell
courses you have gained a knowledge of these ingredients and of how
to feed them to the boys under your care in the proportions laid down.

In my travels round the world the sight of a Gilwell scarf—and I
meet them in many out-of-the-way places—thrills me and fills me
with confidence because I know that the lore which he spreads in ever
widening circles among those around him will be the lore of true
Scouting.

This is not to say that in Scouting there is not adventure unlimited,
because there is. There is hardly any good thing, new, unusual,
original, exciting, that cannot be introduced into Scouting, provided
always that the basic ingredients are right since they are the ones that
have proved themselves for fifty years and more.

Character development is what we are all out for, whether in
Scouting or Guiding, and character, after all, is the only piece of
equipment that any of us will carry with us when we embark on the
greatest adventure of all.

It has been a great joy to be with you this weekend to wish you god-
speed in your continuing of the adventure of Scouting.

*　　　*　　　*

This is not a chronological sequence of events in the life of the Chief
Guide; a list of her flights can be found in the end of the book by those
interested in facts and figures: but here the author has merely tried to
pick out some of the highlights of her travels in the tours which have
meant so much to the children of the world.

1960 had been another particularly eventful year. The World

Conference in Greece was opened by Queen Frederica and the time filled with happy and useful talk, visits to the Parthenon, parties at the Embassies and a reception by the King, Queen and Crown Prince (a former Cub and now Chief Scout) and parties and rallies everywhere— a very happy time.

Later that year Olave went to Switzerland for events at "Our Chalet" and on to Finland to see ten thousand Scouts and Guides at Helsinki. Back to her home perch for a few weeks and then to Denmark for a camp of two thousand Guides and a Rally of ten thousand in the huge stadium at Odense.

There is one sad cloud over the gathering, in that the Queen who has been Chairman of the Committee for the whole two years of planning of this big event, is in hospital with an ulcer, and cannot be seen at all—which is rather sad, as not only has she done so much and is so nice, but you know how people like meeting a *Queen*. She went down with it just this very week, which is so disappointing and such bad luck.

It was an important year in England too, because the British Guides were celebrating their Golden Jubilee with special events everywhere, culminating in a great "Jubilee Pageant" at the Empire Pool, Wembley, where a thousand performers took part in a spectacular pageant "The Journey of Soy" and a "Carnival of Badges" under the direction of Norman Ayrton.

Other countries which had started Guiding at the same time were also celebrating the Jubilee, including Canada where the Guides had planted a golden trail of tulips which stretched across the Dominion from the Atlantic to the Pacific.

Later, the Chief Guide flew to Nigeria for the Independence ceremonies, and inspected Guides at Port Harcourt, Ibadan, Enugo and Lagos—in which latter place she opened the new Guide Headquarters and the Archbishop of Canterbury blessed it. Princess Alexandra was representing the Queen on this occasion "and doing it very well", and there were State Banquets, a Tattoo, and then at midnight the ceremony of lowering the Union Jack and hoisting Nigeria's National Flag,

and this vast territory becomes a self-governing sovereign state—

though still a member of the Commonwealth. A fine speech from the Premier, and then fireworks. A Cathedral service with Archbishops, Bishops, and the Princess. Thence to Kano, where we drive through this amazing walled city of teeming thousands, goats, donkeys, fowls, all mixed with naked children and looking very biblical and hundreds of years behind, though they have electric light and cinemas. Talked with Guides—translated into Hausa—and had an audience with the Emir in his mud-walled Palace.

Then home to Britain for a week or two and after that to Germany to visit the Guides whose fathers were serving with the British Forces, and so, at the end of the year to Pakistan and India, with Miss Helen McSwiney as her travelling companion.

One day's programme in West Pakistan will give some idea of the pace at which the World Chief Guide lived during this long tour.

Monday Dec. 20th 1960. This has been quite a busy day. We did this:

8.30 Wrote some letters.

9.00 Breakfast.

10.00 Set off and visited a Deaf and Dumb School, with Scouts playing games, a bag-pipe band, etc. etc. Tea with the staff. This was in a slum area.

11.00 Rush on to see an amazing Blind School.

12.00 More tea with the Principal of the Girls' College with eleven hundred young girl pupils. Talked to a group of a hundred of them as they may start a Guide Club.

1.00 On to see marvellous "Shalima Gardens" laid out like Versailles by Shah Jehan in 1645—miles of marble stairs, etc. and fountains playing. Here we had a "cook-out" lunch prepared by Guiders. Ate largely and then talked with the forty or so Commissioners and Guides sitting under lovely trees.

3.00 Hurry back to Government House, to be taken round the huge property, to see two schools, maternity clinic, etc. and the farm area. They have two hundred employees and look after their numerous progeny well.

4.00 Hare off to a very important tea with the Community

Development Committee and Council—men and women—
and give them an impassioned address which they lapped
down well.

6.00 Rush off from that to a Press Conference in the Guide House
of about thirty very nice Press men reporters who also lapped
down all I had to say and then asked questions.

7.00 Go round the Guide House where they have the thirteen
Guider trainees living, and then back here to finish all the
rest of my thank letters before going to bed, and off tomorrow
at eight o'clock.

I think that isn't a bad day's work, do you, but they are being so
sweet and it really is wonderful to be able to help them and to give
them this pat on the back. Helen is being absolutely excellent and first-
rate in every way.

Karachi was a most interesting place to visit, a huge busy town of
unbelievable contrasts; sumptuous buildings and tall sky-scrapers for
the big businesses, and then squalor—hundreds of people living like
animals, and certainly not in nearly such good conditions as most
animals in England.

But here the Guides were able to offer a helping hand in many ways,
and the thing that impressed the Chief Guide most about them was their
sense of service to the community.

The outstanding thing about Guides in this country is their
courageous efforts for helping the poor and illiterate backward
women right in the middle of this unspeakable filth and poverty.
They have started tiny little "community centres" where they teach
reading, writing, sewing and other skills to a mixture of young girls
and old women who have never had any education at all. There is no
compulsory State education in Pakistan, so these Guides have got
hold of tiny houses set in the midst of the very poorest parts of the
city, and here they do their teaching. I visited three of these schools
where pupils of different ages—sometimes women of sixty and over—
are learning for the first time the subjects that English children begin
at the age of five. This is known as a "Literacy Project" and it is being
undertaken under very great difficulties but the Guides are carrying
it on with splendid spirit and enthusiasm.

They have also started a "Garden Project" for growing flowers and vegetables in little patches of ground that would otherwise be just sand and dust. These little plots have to be watered twice a day in that hot dusty country but with great care they are managing to grow lettuces, carrots, turnips and cabbages.

In East Pakistan, divided from West Pakistan by a thousand miles of India, the Chief Guide found just the same spirit when she visited it after her time in India.

East Pakistan has faced some troublous times, and one that the whole of our Guide Movement remembers with pride is the cholera epidemic, when the East Pakistan Guides learned how to inoculate people against the disease and then went into the poor homes where they could not let a man come (being Moslems and still in many cases wearing veils when they go out in public). The Guides inoculated altogether seven thousand people and thus helped to prevent the epidemic from spreading—a very fine effort, doing work that could not have been either easy or pleasant to undertake.

From West Pakistan the Chief Guide crossed into India on Christmas Day, and she was delighted to be able to bring together at the barrier the Chief Guide of Pakistan who was seeing her off, and the Chief Guide of India, who was meeting her—an unprecedented occasion for those countries.

How dramatically the scene in India had changed since Olave's former visits. By 1960 not only was there a woman at the head of affairs in the whole of India, but there was also a woman—Mrs Lakshmi Mazumdar—at the head of both the Boy Scout and Girl Guide Movement.

Awaiting the Chief Guide's arrival was a great National Scout and Guide Jamboree at Bangalore.

My first function was to go to the Palace of the Governor of the State of Mysore—His Highness Sri Jayachamaraj Wadiyar who, though of the very old former "royal" family, has renounced his royal status and been appointed Governor under the republican regime. Dressed in flowing white robes and scarlet turban he received us in his gorgeous rooms, and then the President of the Guides in India,

Mrs Ammu Swaminathan, made a speech making him Patron of the Movement in his own State while the Scout and Guide officials who were there in uniform stood round in a half circle. We then all renewed our Promise and Dr Kunzru, the National Scout Commissioner, hung the Patron's decoration round the neck of our very tall large host and was handed a Scout badge to pin on his coat, to complete his enrolment into this new high office!

At this great Jamboree there were twelve and a half thousand in camp, of whom three thousand were Guides, camping on their own separate site. By day the usual happy Jamboree activities went on, and each evening the camp fires gleamed and glowed in the ten camps—six for Scouts and four for Guides—which comprised the whole. The Chief Guide was able to visit the Guides' camp fires:

> I am so glad I did for never have I seen better stunts or more beautiful dancing, sometimes by a team of ten or more, in other cases by just two Guides doing some specially beautiful dance. One dance might depict a stirring incident in history, another might be springtime or a wedding or a journey. And all this was thousands of eager Guides sitting round the blazing fire under a lovely full moon. These camp fires have given me something very special to remember. I know that in lots of countries we have jolly good camp fires, but the standard of these Indian ones was about the best and highest that I have ever seen.

After the Jamboree, the Chief Guide went to Delhi, where, among other engagements, was breakfast and a talk with Mr Nehru.

The Independence Day anniversary celebrations, which the Queen was to attend, included a Scout and Guide Rally for Her Majesty, and this event enabled the Chief Guide for once to be a spectator at a Rally—something which does not often fall to her lot.

On this great day for the Bharat Scouts and Guides the Queen and the Duke of Edinburgh inspected the camp ground and saw their Exhibition and the various units at work, and then watched displays by Scouts and Guides on the rally ground, and met and talked with their leaders.

Then came "Independence Day" itself when the Queen and the

Duke attended a wonderful parade—rather like a Coronation procession and with about four million people looking on. The Chief Guide watched this parade, entranced, for three hours.

As well as the Army, the Navy, and the Air Force, there were lots of elephants and camels in the procession and beautifully decorated "floats". There were thousands of schoolchildren in "blocks" of about a hundred each, each block dressed differently, and folk dancers who came dancing along and stopped in front of the Queen, and many other lovely colourful things to look at. The Queen and the President arrived in State and the Queen's Escort of Mounted Lancers was very fine.

Then to Agra to see the Guides and to gaze for a time at the wonderful Taj Mahal.

It was an immensely interesting experience to Olave, to be travelling round India again and to be staying with Governors and Presidents in their houses which she had known in the old days of the British Raj.

We stayed at the lovely huge Government House in Madras, in a big park full of deer and wonderful gardens. We had a wing to ourselves but did twice meet our host, the Governor, who was in jail for thirteen months when—as an ardent Gandhi-ite—he took part in all that campaign for freeing India from England. Such a charming clever little man too, and we got on like a house on fire.

The Governor of Kerala too, Giri by name, was in jail for four years, and when he was in England they deported him and took away all his diaries which he has never been able to get back. He made one of the finest speeches about Scouting that I have ever heard, was most charming and welcoming, and backs us up to the hilt.

Olave has spent "Thinking Day" (her joint birthday with the Founder) in many different places round the world. During this tour she donned an Indian sari and officially "opened" the newly-built "Baden-Powell Guide Bhavan" at Pachmarhi, in the hills, in a cool climate about three thousand feet above sea level.

We began the day at the camp where about forty Rangers and forty Rovers were assembled in a circle to start the great *Think* from here, catching it as it came across the sea from New Zealand and Australia and speeding it on its way to Europe.

A Guide read a prayer for the Christians, and a Hindu, a Sikh, and a Moslem followed. Then we all thought quietly *to* ourselves and *for* the rest of the world. It was so beautiful, all of us standing there, surrounded by lovely trees, the birds twittering, the sun blazing down from a cloudless sky. And there—high on the hill—was our Guide House waiting for me to come and open it—a super Guide/Scout house and camp ground of over fifty acres—now opening its doors and its land for other countries to come to, as well as for the training of India's own Scouts and Guides and their gallant leaders.

From Burma:

The Rally here in the Government House Garden was lovely and most cheering. This is the same Government House that we both stayed in in 1921—a huge vast enormous palace of a place, and it is lucky for Burma now that the British did *build big*. It makes an ideal and sumptuous Palace for their President—who was most pleasant in my interview with him, and had of course himself been a Scout. So also had the Speaker of their Parliament who came to the Rally.

In Ceylon there were more days filled with hectic work and many engagements. The Chief Guide stayed with the Prime Minister, Mrs Bandaranaika, where Lord Attlee was a fellow guest. "We don't match *very* well, he is rather old and tired, but he was Prime Minister when Ceylon got its independence and is being feted for that."

The long round of official dinners, on top of all her Guide work, was rather exhausting, and after a visit to Rome, an audience with the Pope ("who shook hands and beamed upon me and said quite a lot in Italian and was very charming and friendly") it was good to be home at Hampers once more.

Linger in bed late. Heavenly not to have to get up hurriedly to catch a plane. Looked through piles of letters but couldn't be bothered to write any, and went in hot sunshine to dig all the afternoon in my garden.

In a farewell message to the Guides and Scouts of India the Chief Guide wrote:

I have not only met thousands of smiling faces, but have also faced several thousand cameras, and each eager photographer always seemed to be anxious to get a picture and then "just one more".

So here is a challenge to you all. Just one more test passed for gaining a badge; just one more recruit to join up with your patrol; just one more Guider or Scouter to be found for just one more Scout Troop or Guide Company, Pack or Flock. Just one more helper and supporter and then, above all, just one more good turn service to the community. Just one more kind thought and prayer that the spirit of Scouting may spread far and wide throughout India.

On July 12th of that year (1961) Her Majesty the Queen opened Baden-Powell House in Queen's Gate, and the Duke of Gloucester unveiled the statue of B-P which stands outside the house.

CHAPTER XVII

East and West

TWENTY-ONE years after his father's death, a second break in the happy B-P family came when at the end of 1962 Peter (the second Lord Baden-Powell) died after twenty-six years of happy married life.

Olave was away in Malaya at the time the news reached her. Peter's death was a great sorrow to his family and friends. He was only forty-nine and had been doing splendid work for Scouting, more particularly with the B-P Guild of Old Scouts; and he had just been awarded the Silver Wolf—British Scouting's highest award.

His widow, Carine Lady Baden-Powell, took his place as President of the Guild.

Peter's son Robert succeeded to the title and, with his wife Patience, has already made a notable contribution to the Movement; as has also Olave's daughter Betty who, with her husband Gervas Clay, forms yet another instance of "double harness" in the B-P Scout and Guide family.

B-P used to tell the story of a dream, where, he said, he died and went to Heaven. St Peter met him at the gate and asked conversationally, "And how did you like Japan?"

"Japan—I never went there."

"Then you can't come in here," said St Peter. "Why do you think God has put you in such a lovely world if you are only going to sit down in one corner of it. Go back, and don't come here until you have done a bit more travelling."

And so B-P went to Japan. And now Olave was paying her first visit to this marvellous country, not so much for the sake of visiting a new place, but because a large part of her big family—at least fifteen thousand of them—lived in that country.

I have not caught up with enough sleep yet after the long flight. It was a grand trip and we enjoyed it, but it was terribly funny that the plane kept to Paris clock time and as we crossed the date line and also kept losing time as we flew westward, our meals came at odd times—the last one being breakfast at three in the afternoon. We didn't actually go over the Pole but skirted it in the dark, and at dawn we landed at Anchorage, seeing Mt. McKinley, the highest mountain on that continent in glorious early sunlight. And there—stopping to re-fuel—I found a bunch of about thirty Girl Scout leaders and Committee members all waiting to greet me. The Air hostess, knowing I was on board, had rung them up half an hour before. It was jolly to find them so unexpectedly there in Alaska—and so amusing to realise that I was back in the U.S.A. again, in their latest joined State—Alaska. Talks, hand-shakes, greetings, happy new friendships made in less than thirty minutes and then off across the northern bit of the Pacific Ocean—to Japan at last.

Though this was her first visit, and she knew not one word of the language, the Chief Guide found herself at once among friends.

We rushed about, hand in hand, doing Press interviews, talks on radio and "T.V.", attended various meetings and paid calls on the high officials of the land.

As a climax to this busy round I was taken to call on the Empress of Japan, in her great Palace; and although we could not speak one another's language at all, we were able, through her lady-in-waiting interpreter, to have quite a conversation, and she expressed her personal sympathy with all that Girl Scouting is doing and appreciates what it can mean to the girls of her nation.

It was not exactly the easiest "conversation piece" with every word having to go to her translator first and then on to her Imperial Majesty, and then her Japanese answer coming back to me in English —everything having to be done in a whisper, out of politeness, that being the custom in such high places!

This was a very special occasion for the Girl Scouts and they had arranged, for the Chief Guide, a splendid Rally of over two thousand in the gymnasium of the Sacred Heart Convent. Their most charming Crown Princess had been a pupil at this school and she came along and joined in the fun.

The whole Rally was splendidly organised, and so that I could see each Guide personally and individually, they were all massed down the sides of the big Hall and at a given signal turned facing away from where I stood at the end, marched forward, wheeled in, and in rows of six came striding up to me holding hands—and I then shook hands with them six at a time, and on they went, divided in half again and passed on back to their places. It was most effective and gave me the chance of receiving rows of smiles in cheery eager friendly faces.

The Brownies wear very short reddish skirts and caps and white shirts and they did a delicious dance game, just like Brownies do everywhere; and the Guide displays were quite lovely, dancing in the real Japanese style to the accompaniment of the quaintest sort of "piano-cum-zither-cum-guitar".

In Tokyo, the biggest city in the world, the Chief Guide saw miles and miles of old buildings mixed in with hundreds of new skyscrapers and huge office blocks. The Emperor's Palace stands in the middle of the city.

In Osaka, where the great "Expo 70" took place in 1970, a Guide meeting was held inside the Osaka Bank which had been specially lent for the occasion, and where all the members of the Bank's Board, with the Mayor and other high officials, were there to greet the Chief Guide. Between the counters of this huge Bank stood rows of Guides and Brownies forming a Guard of Honour and holding up the business of the Bank while the managers and clerks waved their hands in greeting and goodwill.

After Japan to Korea, Okinawa, Taiwan, Hong-Kong, Malaya and Thailand—a strenuous journey, catching planes at unearthly hours, sometimes with sleepless nights, always with busy days.

Sometimes she must wonder whether it is all worth while, and why she keeps on doing it. But then some quite unexpected word of gratitude and encouragement comes to sustain her—as in this letter from Korea:

Today we are very much obliged to you and to Lord Baden-Powell for your high spirit that has made millions of girls of all nations, races, customs and religions to follow the same Promise and Laws together and share friendship with one another.

In Korea there are still many who have not been granted to take part of the Scout spirit . . . We promise to try to extend your spirit to our neighbours. Now we are all standing together around the World Flag with a candle light in each hand as a symbol of human love. Here we say our sincere wishes for our sisters near and far while the flame is sparkling. Wishing you to visit us before not too long, we pray for your health.

If it was St Peter who sent B-P to Japan, it was this letter that sent the Chief Guide hot-foot to Korea and made the journey seem worthwhile.

There may still be one State in the United States of America that Olave has not visited; there are certainly not more. She has countless friends in almost every part of that vast continent, to whom she loves to return, like a homing bird, whenever the Boy Scouts or the Girl Scouts invite her to carry out some worthwhile project for the advancement or encouragement of their Movement.

Whether in Washington or New York, Rochester, Chicago, or indeed wherever her travels take her, Olave knows that a comfortable bed awaits her and that a group of intimate friends will gather round her as soon as she sets foot on Kennedy Airport; they will all want to welcome her and to hear her latest news, for, though she keeps up a constant correspondence with them all, there is nothing like the touch of a hand— or a cheek—and not even the frequent telephone calls across the Atlantic can quite take the place of these personal visits.

Three developments that have taken place in the last decade have not only given her immense pleasure but have forged an even deeper link in the chain which binds her to the Boy Scout movement in that country.

First—what she calls her "Magic Carpet"—the gift of a Credit Card which takes her anywhere in the world, free of cost to herself. It was presented to her as a truly generous gesture by the Executive Board of the Boy Scouts of America in appreciation of what she has done, and is doing, for American and World Scouting.

Secondly, the best biography of her famous husband ever to be written comes from the pen of an American, William Hillcourt, who, as a Boy Scout in Denmark in the early days of the Scout Movement, has the advantage not only of being a first-rate author but also of having known the Founder personally for many years. His book *Baden-Powell—the Two Lives of a Hero* was written after an immense amount of research and with Olave's full co-operation and assistance.

And thirdly, at New Brunswick, beside the National Headquarters of the Boy Scouts of America, stands today the Johnston Historical Museum. Here is to be found the whole history of Scouting from its early beginning on Brownsea Island to the present day (the latter exemplified by a full-scale replica of a spaceship manned by former Scouts).

Here, too, is to be found a "Baden-Powell Room", containing many of the Founder's own possessions, writings and sketches, to be available for study by Scouts of every land for generations to come. Here is a life-size wax figure of him sitting at his desk at Pax Hill, Bentley, planning for the Movement which has had such influence on the world.

Olave has contributed much to this museum, for she realises that here is the place where Scouts of the future will best be able to study the ideas and ideals of their Founder as well as of their national Scout leaders and heroes.

All the exhibits in this museum are carefully preserved, beautifully mounted and displayed to the fullest advantage, no trouble or expense having been spared in building up a unique collection for posterity.

It is a magnificent museum, and its far-seeing and generous donor, the late Mr Gale Johnston, will rank as one of the greatest benefactors to Scouting of all time.

Olave makes no secret of her love for the United States and for so many of her citizens.

It needs to be far better understood on this side of the Atlantic, for behind and beyond the façade of newspaper publicity regarding its trials and tribulations lies a nation of vigorous forceful splendid people, living grand sound lives, building fine good homes, and with hearts that are generous and kind to the umpteenth degree. Never do I feel greater warmth of welcome anywhere, and the eagerness with which one is made to feel at home is both touching and heart-warming. I am thrilled anew every time I see and hear and share in their Scouting activities, and only wish that every one of you could have shared some of the experiences that I have had there which have been so uplifting, so stimulating and encouraging.

The love is certainly not all on one side. Olave has enshrined herself in the hearts of Americans, young and old, and by mutual correspondence and visits the friendships are kept alive.

Britain, Germany, and other countries have had great opportunities in the last few years of learning more about their young neighbours across the Herring Pond, by the fact of the presence among them of so many Service personnel and their children. Where there are children there are inevitably Boy Scouts and Girl Scouts, with the American Girl Scout Movement calling its thousands of units by the name of TOFS (i.e. Troops on Foreign Soil). These have received many visits from the Chief Guide and have been welcomed into the camps and activities of the Guides of the home country. As they return to their homes in every part of the United States many of them carry back with them happy memories of friendships made over the camp fire, as well as of personal visits to the Chief Guide in her home at Hampton Court Palace.

Such experiences cannot fail to speed up mutual understanding and appreciation of each other's way of life.

*　　*　　*

When a long tour round Africa was being planned, the Chief Guide issued to those concerned a little summary of what she likes—and what she does not like—on such tours.

The "likes" of course include seeing and talking to the Guides, meeting and talking with their leaders and with supporters of the Movement; talking on World Guiding to the general public, Press, radio, etc., and to those connected with Education, the Churches, and other representative people, to arouse where needed their fuller interest and co-operation.

She also likes having, now and then, a whole free day for catching up with correspondence; and in her semi-retirement she likes to go to bed early and not to have to start life too early in the morning.

What she hopes not to have to do is to attend many ordinary social functions which have no connection with, or value for, the Movement—time being so limited and the purpose of her visit being the advancement of Guiding.

Having already visited most of the world's beauty spots and places of historical interest in earlier days, she no longer wants to be taken "sight-seeing".

She does not like addressing "mixed" audiences of adults and children at public meetings, as she feels that she cannot speak fully of Guiding's more serious aspects if the children themselves are there.

She asks not to have presents, for by experience she has found that, if one is given, other people are apt to feel that they should follow suit, and this makes an impossible situation.

"No flowers by request", as these do not "match" uniform; no planting of trees, if possible, as the view usually taken by photographers of such incidents, and subsequently published, is apt to be very inelegant! No autographs to be asked for. If one is given, others will certainly be demanded, and then she is sunk! Very special log-books or programmes come under a different category, but cannot be signed in public.

Once an itinerary and programme has been approved she asks that no "extras" should be added in at the last minute if this can be avoided.

These are requests, not in any sense "orders" and they are thrown out as suggestions in order to make things easier for all concerned.

CHAPTER XVIII

The Home Office

IT was said during the Second World War, that it required two hundred men on the ground to keep one man in the air.

The Chief Guide, who spends so much of her time in the air, has a "ground staff" consisting of the Director and the people who run the World Bureau in London and the Chief Commissioner and her staff who run Commonwealth Headquarters in Buckingham Palace Road.

She also has a "Home Office Staff" at Hampton Court Palace, comprising her housekeeper and the daily workers who keep her apartment going, and volunteer secretaries, car drivers, and assistant gardeners, who come along as required to help in typing her letters, addressing her hundreds of Christmas card envelopes, furnishing and planting her roof garden, and carrying her hither and thither in their own cars. These people are all only too pleased and proud to give their time and service in enabling their Chief to fly round and inspire the great Movement for which she stands.

Her apartment—"Hampers" as it is known to her family—has been variously described as a home from home, a hotel, or—as she says—a railway station, judging by the numbers of people who come in and out, parking their baggage or possessions, meeting their children from school, taking off from Heathrow or meeting people there, or staying for weeks while they house-hunt in the home counties.

Of the many stately homes in which Olave has lived, Hampton Court Palace is doubtless the stateliest. This historic pile was built in the reign of Henry VIII by Thomas Wolsey, Archbishop of York, on a site which he acquired on lease in 1514 from the Order of St John of Jerusalem.

In 1515 Wolsey became a Cardinal and Lord Chancellor of England, and as his power increased so also did his riches. His country house on the banks of the Thames was already rivalling a royal palace in magnificence, with its two hundred and fifty richly furnished guest-rooms and a household staff of some five hundred.

When, in 1527, a treaty was signed between France and England, the French Ambassador and his suite of four hundred were entertained at Hampton Court at Wolsey's expense.

But power corrupts and Wolsey's power was already waning when he had his difference with the King, and in a desperate attempt to regain the royal favour he handed over to Henry his Manor of Hampton Court with all its buildings and furnishings, its tapestry and its plate. But in vain. On October 30th 1529 all his lands and goods were seized and though he received a general pardon in 1530 and retired to his province of York, he was arrested in November for high treason and died while on his way to face his trial in London.

So now the King was in sole possession and he at once set to work to enlarge Hampton Court and brought to live there in turn five of his six wives, Anne Boleyn, Jane Seymour, Anne of Cleves, Catharine Howard, and Catharine Parr.

Henry's children, Edward VI (born here), Mary I and Elizabeth I, each held Court at the Palace and here James I presided over the Conference for the determining of things said to be "amiss in the Church" and approved the authorised version of the Bible.

Charles I lived here as King and, for a short time, as prisoner during the Civil War, and after his death, when other royal possessions were sold by Order of Parliament, Hampton Court Palace was retained for the use of the Protector, Oliver Cromwell.

Charles II repaired the Palace after the Restoration and remade the gardens; but for some reason his brother James II never lived in the place.

Then in 1699 came William and Mary and there began a great re-building. Wolsey's palace was by now nearly two hundred years old and the King decided to modernise and commissioned Sir Christopher Wren to plan a new building. Many designs were drawn up, some of which involved the destruction of everything already there with the single exception of the Great Hall. But, owing to the death of Queen Mary in 1694, this wholesale plan was abandoned and, when a fall from his horse led, in 1702, to King William's death, all building came to an end and so, fortunately for us, much of the beautiful Tudor work remains.

Queen Anne and the first two Georges held Court in the new part of the Palace but after George II's death in 1760 the Palace was abandoned as a royal residence. The state rooms were opened to the public and nearly a thousand rooms were set aside as "Grace and Favour" apartments, to be lent by the Sovereign to the widows or children of those who had rendered distinguished service to the Crown. Occasionally the loan is to the distinguished man himself, as in the case of the late Lord Birdwood; but normally the only male tenants are the Chaplain and the staff.

Of these thousand rooms, Olave Lady Baden-Powell occupies sixteen, eight in her main apartment and eight in an annexe.

Of the thousands of visitors who throng the grounds and the state apartments of the Palace each year, only a very small proportion ever see the inside of the private apartments. This is natural because their residents are for the most part elderly and retired and only when they have young relations or friends to stir them up does one see any young people in their vicinity.

Olave's apartment is an exception to the general rule, for not only do her eight grandchildren frequent the place but, owing to her unique position in a "youth" Movement, she receives in the course of any one year a very large number of young Scout and Guide visitors.

When she took up residence in 1942 she was only fifty-three and was the "baby" among her fellows, some of whom were in their nineties. Though the twenty-eight years have corrected this, she is still probably the busiest and most energetic person there, and the one who receives the largest number of visitors.

Of Queen Anne it was recorded by Alexander Pope that on her visits to Hampton Court Palace she "sometimes counsel took and sometimes tea".

The same might be said of some of the hundreds of people who visit the Chief Guide.

At one end of her long drawing-room, furnished with the lovely old walnut chests, presentation writing tables, and other treasures from Pax Hill, as well as gifts from many parts of the world, the Chief Guide sits every day at her typewriter—always with an eye on the clock to see how much time she has before guests arrive for lunch or tea.

Never having been professionally trained as a typist she is inclined to be rather hard on her machine, bits of which have an awkward habit of flying off or twisting themselves up at the wrong moment. She must, in her time, have worn out an immense number of typewriters—which travel as constantly as she does—and "Mr Babro" is a frequent visitor to the apartment with a machine for her to try out while he takes away the current invalid in exchange. Sometimes another typewriter will be clacking beside her as a joint effort is made to deal with her enormous mail. This end of the room is the "office".

Visitors for "counsel and tea" are often upon her before her desk has been cleared, and Olave will then cross to the other side of the room where the tea-table waits, and give her unhurried attention to her guests, often returning for several hours, later in the evening, to her typewriter. Tea-time has always been a favourite and relaxing moment and each visitor can be sure of her undivided interest and sympathetic concern for his or her affairs. Olave herself will usually drink only cup after cup of weak sweet tea while urging her guests towards bread and jam, sandwiches and cakes.

Her bed-room—reputed to have been used as a green room by William Shakespeare when preparing to act in the Great Hall just below ("The question is do I sleep in Shakespeare's dressing-room, or did he dress in my bedroom?") is even larger than the drawing-room and a corner turret—an old powdering closet—holds her husband's books, medals and other treasures. The walls of every room are adorned with his delightful water-colours, reminiscent of their joint visits to many lands, and in the long hall, underneath his portrait, is one of his sculptures—"The Blind Slave". In a case on the wall are his presentation swords, and though many relics have been distributed to Army and Scout Museums there are still enough historical items to keep a visitor busy for a long time.

In cupboards in the drawing-room are the dozens of scrap-books, made by Olave as a "spare-time activity" and filled with pictures, photographs, sketches, cuttings, and other interesting mementoes of tours and of Scout and Guide events in many parts of the world.

The Chief Guide is fortunately gifted with a keen sense of humour which comes to her assistance in some of the less glamorous episodes in her life. She is a grand raconteuse and usually has some fresh story to tell, very often against herself.

She is somewhat "accident-prone", due probably to the speed with which she travels. Running down a flight of stairs in one of the Guide training houses, she fell heavily and cracked three ribs. She was immensely tickled to hear a voice call out—"Oh, it's only you, I was afraid it was the new Hoover."

Incidentally, on this occasion, the Chief Guide finished all that she had to do and travelled many miles home before she put herself to bed and discovered from the doctor the cause of her pain. She makes light of such incidents and scorns the idea of bed unless and until it is absolutely necessary.

The big difference in age between her and her famous husband has led to some amusing if slightly embarrassing incidents. Bicycling from her apartment to her garden one day she saw a couple reading the plaque bearing her name at the foot of her staircase. "Lady Baden-Powell!" one of them exclaimed. "She must have been dead for years." And the smiling cyclist pursued her way.

On another occasion, when in her most energetic seventies, she was visiting an island famous for its beautiful gardens, she was touched to find a bath-chair awaiting her pleasure.

A weary-looking couple, on a hot summer day, stopped her as she went along in her gardening outfit, and asked her who lived in the various apartments.

"I live in one of them," Olave replied and asked whether they would like to come in and be refreshed with a cup of tea. The invitation was readily accepted and while she was making the tea, to carry along to the visitors, their attention was caught by the name "Baden-Powell" on an envelope.

"Any relation?" they asked, awe-struck.

"Yes, I'm his wife."

Consternation, gasps, and then it came out: "We didn't know you were still alive!"

Another garden incident suggested to the Rev. John Bailey a text for an address that he gave to the Guides at their Thinking Day service in Norwich Cathedral.

Some years ago my wife and I went to visit Hampton Court Palace. After a happy time there we wanted to go home a different way through the Park. We didn't know if this was permissible so we decided to ask a lady we saw in a cotton dress, with gloves on, gardening. She could not have been more helpful. With a friendly smile she told us that we could go through the Park, pointed out the way and told us the number of the bus we could catch on the other side which would take us home. We thanked her and walked away. In a minute my wife said, "Do you know I believe that was Lady Baden-Powell, the Chief Guide," and of course she was right. Following her clear directions we had a most glorious walk on an evening I shall never forget . . . Now Guides she has given all of *you* clear directions to follow through your lives so that you may make them glorious.

In her gardening clothes the Chief Guide loves to be incognito and to move freely among the thousands of visitors who throng this historic place.

But when it is a case of Scout or Guide visitors she naturally likes to be warned well in advance so that she may be tidy in uniform, and the "droppers-in" do not always receive that cordial welcome which comes to expected guests. For, as all busy people know, it is not easy, when just leaving to catch a plane, dressing for an occasion, or hurrying to finish letters for the post, to welcome the "just-passing-by-saw-your-name-thought-I-would-look-in" type of caller. Olave is sometimes inclined to "blow up". "*Why* didn't you let me know?" she will say. "I would have loved to give you a meal but now I'm afraid I can't give you even a minute. You should have telephoned or written beforehand."

This is a very understandable attitude because where dozens, and sometimes hundreds, of visitors are entertained in one week, it is necessary for her, as well as for her housekeeper, to make plans in advance—even if it is only for tea.

Her housekeeper, cook, and devoted friend, Mrs Searle, who has been with Olave for seventeen years, tells an amusing story of her initiation.

"Will the work be heavy?" she enquired, when applying at the employment agency for the appointment. "Oh no," was the reply, "it's just for one elderly lady living alone—probably just means light meals on a tray."

It was not many days before the truth was revealed, but Mrs Searle, as a Girl Guide in Ireland in the very early days, had obviously learned to "Be Prepared" for what is a fairly strenuous career. But she would not change it for anything. "Never a dull moment," she says, and never was a truer word spoken.

About once a month, when she is in residence, Olave will give what she describes as a "Finger Lunch" party, when guests from all ends of the earth—people who may never have met each other before but who are all her friends—assemble at little tables for four or six in the large drawing-room, to lunch off sherry or tomato juice, sandwiches and rolls, with a sweet and coffee to follow.

While they are enjoying their lunch Olave will get up from the table and "introduce" them to one another by name, explaining where each one comes from, how and where they met, and what he or she does or is specially interested in.

The chances are that before the meal is over several people will have discovered either that they were at school together, or are related to one another in some way, or at least have mutual friends; and so the ball of friendship rolls on and nothing delights Olave more than to know that it was in her home that a lasting friendship was made or a new recruit caught for some task within the Movement.

A lunch party on July 3rd 1969, for instance, included visitors from Bangalore, Bombay, Barbados, Liberia, Malaysia, Tasmania, Kenya, Finland and Majorca. This is typical of many others. Mixed in with these assorted visitors are usually a few of her co-residents in the Palace—all with interesting lives behind them and many still carrying on useful service for the community in one direction or another.

With each visitor Olave herself has some special personal link and each must have a quiet talk with her during or after lunch. Scrap-books will be brought out and browsed over, and by the time all this has happened lunch-time will often be overtaken by tea-time, but, as she says, it is all so worthwhile, this making and cementing of friendships. Like the late Archbishop of Cape Town she is colour-blind and her friends are of every nationality, creed, and colour.

Guests are bidden for half-past twelve, in order that the daily staff who prepare and serve the meal may not be delayed too long over the clearing away; and woe betide the late-comers who explain that the traffic on the road held them up. "There is always traffic on the road," their hostess will observe, "and one has to allow for it". But they are quickly forgiven and fed with lunch, no matter how grave their crime.

The Chief Guide does feel irritated by latecomers because she herself can never afford to be late. Her programmes are scheduled to the last minute and her own solution of the traffic problem is to arrive at her destination far too early, rather than a minute late, and then to hover hidden round some convenient corner until the precise moment when she is expected on the rally ground or in the hall. It would be as bad for her to "arrive" too early as too late, military precision is what is required of her and what she usually manages to achieve.

On one occasion, in a foreign country, her plane did the unusual thing of arriving an hour before time. Her agitated host met her and carried her away to his house where he concealed her until the time of her expected arrival. He then got her back to the Airport just as the Guard of Honour, the Town Band, the Fire Brigade, the Mayor, and all the rest, were in position, and she "arrived" once more with due ceremony and was officially welcomed.

The lunch parties are great fun, but there is a limit to the number of people who are free at that time of day or who can be fitted in. So it is often tea or supper instead of lunch.

Then rather a different sort of party happens when a group of Scouts, Guides, or leaders from another country book themselves to call upon her. Hampton Court is on the itinerary of most visiting groups "doing" Europe and some of these frequently plan to call in and meet their Chief in person. She has a roof garden, bright throughout the summer with geraniums and other flowers and furnished with plenty of seats and tables which are in frequent use during the tourist season. These groups will be invited inside to look at the Founder's watercolours which adorn the walls, and to see the dozens of scrap-books, in which they will often find photographs of their countries and even of themselves. This will be followed by refreshments, a little talk from their hostess and left hand-shakes all round and, of course, the production of cameras before they go on their way.

Across the roof garden Olave has her other eight rooms in what is known as her "Annexe". Here are beds, bath and kitchen, for the use of friends or relations when the apartment overflows, or for visiting Scout

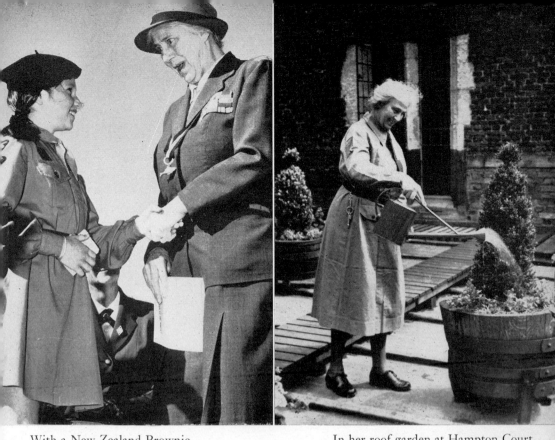

With a New Zealand Brownie,
April, 1967

In her roof garden at Hampton Court

With Guides in Tokyo, 1966

At home, Hampton Court Palace, with her daughter Betty

At the Albert Hall, Stirling, Scotland, 1962

or Guide families from overseas who want to see the sights of London but for whom hotel accommodation may be a problem.

It was in the year that Elizabeth II was crowned that the Guides decided to do an extra good turn in her honour, as a Coronation Tribute to one who had herself been a keen Guide. As her personal tribute Lady Baden-Powell chose the furnishing, camp fashion, of those extra rooms which up to that time had only been used for storing luggage. She foresaw that London would be overcrowded, and in the event nearly three hundred people spent nights in the Annexe, near enough to London to enable them to share in the excitement of Coronation Year. Though she herself saw the Coronation from a privileged position she had far greater satisfaction in feeling that she had enabled so many others to have their share of the fun, for Olave is a born "sharer".

Coronation Year, with all its special events and extra numbers of visitors was a very busy one for Guiding and for Olave, both at home and throughout the country where Coronation Tributes and Coronation Rallies were the theme.

Besides being a "mother of millions", as well as a grandmother in her own right, Olave is also god-mother to a large number of children and ex-children, and she continues to interest herself in their well-being long after they have arrived at years of discretion. Some god-parents have a way of forgetting the children for whom they have accepted responsibility once the "silver mug" period is past; but Olave likes to do things thoroughly and to keep in touch, in after life, with as many as possible of these babies. On a shelf in Hampers is a large album, with a page or pages allocated to each god-child, whether hers or B-P's, and into this she pastes photographs of them at different stages, from babyhood upwards, news about their education, confirmation, careers, marriages, and children. To collect all this information from the parents of some forty babies, or later from the god-children themselves, entails quite a large amount of correspondence and labour, but to this unique god-parent it is a labour of love.

When, on her birthday in 1967, Olave gave a "family" party in London, inviting all her children, grandchildren, cousins and in-laws to a fork luncheon at the Guide Club, she also included the god-children.

It was a party of about eighty, many of whom had never met one another before, and was a really happy gathering of the clans, with Olave

M

for once in plain clothes and not surrounded by uniformed Guides.

But she atoned for this shocking "lapse from duty" by attending a Guide birthday tea-party at Commonwealth Headquarters later in the day.

CHAPTER XIX

Be Happy

THIS farewell message to the Girl Guides was found among the papers left by their Founder:

My dear Guides,

This is just a farewell note to you, the last that you will have from me.

It is just to remind you, when I have passed on, that your business in life is to be happy and to make others happy.

That sounds comfortable and easy, doesn't it?

You begin making other people happy by doing Good Turns to them. You need not worry about making *yourselves* happy, as you will very soon find that that comes by itself. When you make other people happy it makes YOU happy too.

Later on, when you have a home of your own, by making it a bright and cheery one you will make your husband a happy man. If all homes were bright and cheery there would be fewer public houses, and the men would not want to go out to them but would stay at home.

It may mean hard work for you but will bring its own reward.

Then if you keep your children healthy and clean and busy they will be happy. Happy children love their parents. And there is nothing that can give you greater joy than a loving child.

I am sure God means us to be happy in this life. He has given us a world to live in that is full of beauties and wonders, and He has given us not only eyes to see them but minds to understand them—if we only have the sense to look at them in that light.

We can enjoy bright sunshine and glorious views. We can see beauty in the trees and flowers. We can watch with wonder how the seed produces the young plant which grows to a flower which, in its turn, will replace other flowers as they die off.

For though plants, like people, die, their race does not die away, but new ones are born and grow up to carry on the Creator's plan.

So, do you see, you women are the chosen servants of God in two ways: first to carry on the race, to bring children into the world to replace the men and women who pass away: secondly, to bring happiness into the world by making happy homes and by being yourselves good cheery comrades for your husbands and children.

And that is where you, as Guides, especially come in. By being a "comrade", that is, by taking an interest in your husband's work and aspirations, you can help him with your sympathy and suggestions and so be a Guide to him. And also, in bringing up your children by strengthening and training their minds and characters, as well as their bodies and health, you will be giving them to the better use and enjoyment of life.

By giving out love and happiness in this way you will gain for yourselves the return love of husband and children—and there is nothing better in this world.

You will then find that Heaven is not the kind of happiness somewhere up in the skies after you are dead, but right here and now, in this world in your own home.

So—Guide others to happiness and you will bring happiness to yourselves: and by doing this you will be doing what God wants of you.

God be with you—Baden-Powell.

"May the wings of your happiness never lose a feather."

That would be the wish of every Scout and Guide, past and present, for Olave Baden-Powell. It is a wish that promises fulfilment. Bent and battered at times these wings may have been, but no feathers have been shed, for their owner is still balanced in full flight, enjoying each adventure as it comes along, and bringing much happiness in her train.

It is not that life has always been gentle with her. She has known knocks. In the course of a long life she has lost father, mother, sister, brother, her beloved husband, her only son, and a favourite grandson, Michael King, who, at the dawn of a promising career, lost his life in an act of self-sacrifice.

And she has, of course, outlived many of her greatest friends.

But happiness is from within and to Olave, as to the Founder, it is part of the duty, as well as the pleasure, of life to be happy. "My great *task* of happiness," wrote R. L. Stevenson, and she would agree with him that to falter in this task is to need forgiveness and a good shot in the arm.

B-P used to say that the richest and happiest person was not the one with the most possessions but the one with the fewest needs, and he was certainly a very rich man who felt that his every need in life had been met.

When the Scouts of the world wanted to give a present to their Founder at the time of the "Coming of Age" Jamboree at Arrowe Park in 1929, Olave was commissioned to find out secretly whether there was anything that B-P specially wanted or that would be an acceptable gift.

She went into his study at Pax Hill and asked him: "If a present was in the air, darling, is there any one thing that you would specially like?"

"Yes," replied her husband, after a minute's thought, "I do rather want a new pair of braces."

The braces—emerald green ones—were presented to him by the Scouts of Ireland, with due ceremony, at the Jamboree, where he also received a Rolls-Royce (Jam Roll), a motor caravan (Eccles), and a fine portrait of himself by David Jagger, R.A.

There are probably few people in the world who have had so much showered upon them in the way of presents—unexpected and unasked for tributes to two very special people. And now Olave has to bear the brunt by herself. She is, on the whole, an unwilling recipient of offerings. She has all that any one person needs and she feels that there are so many people in the world whose needs are greater.

While she appreciates the thought that prompts the desire to give, the tangible outcome can sometimes be an embarrassment, especially when she is on the move. Sometimes, indeed, she may seem almost ungracious in her rejection of offerings—"No, I don't have presents, keep it or give it to someone who needs it."

Yet it is in the nature of people to wish to shower presents on those they love and revere, and it is one of the problems that have to be faced when you have thousands of young admirers.

When the gift is one of money it can often be ploughed back into Guiding in some special way, as in the case of the Ice Cream Fund. Having firmly rejected any idea of presents before arriving on Australian soil, the Chief Guide hoped that she had made her meaning clear; but, nothing daunted, the Guides in Australia devised a plan. Each Guide was told that, when buying an ice-cream for herself, she might also "buy" one for the Chief Guide; and that instead of transmitting the sticky melting stuff in kind she might send its cost in pennies to a central fund.

This resulted of course in many hundreds of pounds finding their way to Olave's bank, to be spent "in any way that she liked"—and she liked very much to use a great deal of this gift in providing translations of Guide literature into their own language for the use of the countries she had visited in South America; and later in giving doors for Guid Headquarters buildings in many parts of the world. Such gifts were sent not from herself personally, but, through her, from their sister Guides in Australia and through the subsequent exchange of letters were the means of new links being formed in the great chain of Guiding round the world. This Ice Cream Fund has become a real "widow's cruse", added to from time to time by admirers near and far who have realised that she wants nothing for herself.

The Chief Guide loves flowers and grows all her own for the house in her allotment garden at Hampton Court. But she does not, on parade, welcome the presentation of bouquets which she feels are not a correct part of uniform, and generally asks beforehand that they should not be given. Where they are presented she is usually quick to find a sick Guide or a near-by hospital to take them off her hands.

Baskets of exotic fruits, books, carvings, pictures, china, glass, and even furniture, have found their way to her at Guide Rallies, and these can be somewhat burdensome appendages when she is on a flying visit and travelling light. Royalty, no doubt, has to face an even greater problem in this respect but then Royalty has an entourage able to cope tactfully with such matters and to save donors and recipients from embarrassment.

The Boy Scouts of America, in 1968, solved their problem of giving in a very practical way. Longing to express their gratitude for what Olave Baden-Powell has done in helping their Boy Scout Movement as well as their girls on her many tours in the United States, they hit upon an idea. She has seldom refused an invitation to attend one of their big national Jamborees and to give them the uplift and encouragement which, as the Founder's wife, she alone can give; and in recognition of this they presented her with a Credit Card on the American Express Company, thus enabling her to travel in comfort, free of cost, on her many overseas journeys. This wonderful gift, her "magic carpet" as Olave calls it, came as a totally unlooked for and unexpected reward. To one who, in earlier days, had spent so much of her own money on travelling, seldom refusing, on grounds of expense, anything that she was asked to do, this gesture brought immense surprise and relief, for it was something which could indeed be ploughed back into the work for which she lives.

When her eightieth birthday was approaching, the Chief Guide could not help wondering what this might have in store for her in the way of plunder; and she cleverly forestalled any plans that might be in the offing by publishing a message explaining her wishes and requirements.

It has come round to me that some people consider one's eightieth birthday to be a rather special date in anybody's life, though to be quite candid I would myself like to forget that I have come to such an advanced age.

Every year I am repeatedly touched by the veritable flood of kindly messages which come to me on Thinking Day, and now I have an idea that this will in all probability happen again. I shall only just have arrived home and there will be an immense amount of mail to catch up with.

So I am going to ask whether, if you were contemplating sending me a message, you would give me a present instead, and something that I would appreciate above everything else. You know, don't you, that the one main love in my life now is for Guiding, and my one chief wish is for its development and further progress on the lines laid down by my husband whose birthday is on the same day as mine.

Our Movement is in good heart, bigger and better than ever before —thanks to the work that is being done by each and every one of its members, and I know that you are all as busy as bees and have plenty of work on your hands.

But most people are allowed on their birthday to have just something a little "extra" in one way or another—so what about this for a present which would make me intensely happy.

One extra Brownie, one extra Guide, one extra Ranger, one extra Guider; one extra Company or Pack; one extra Good Turn; one extra penny or pound for the World Friendship Fund; one extra prayer that Guiding may grow, and with your own personal effort continue to grow, in strength and happy success in the year to come.

If each one of you, in your own particular sphere, could do just that—in addition to what you are already doing—my birthday would be indeed the most joyous of days and my happiness would be complete.

There is every indication of the fact that this birthday wish is being granted in very many, if not all, parts of the world.

CHAPTER XX

What is She Like?

"ALL my own growing," says Olave, rushing in from her garden with arms and baskets full of lilies of the valley, roses, or other fragrant bunches from her allotment in the Park. She is as enthusiastic about these flowers—and her bundles of rhubarb—and as proud of them as if they were "all her own" Guides and Scouts, and cares for them just as vigorously, for to her to do a thing at all means to do it as thoroughly as possible.

The most vital people that one knows are by no means the easiest to describe. Neither the printed word nor the artist's pencil seems the right medium for reproducing a sparkle and radiance which have little to do with black lettering or even coloured portraiture.

"She has no face, only an expression," said one artist who tried to paint Olave.

She is so very much more alive than most people. To try a description in print is rather like trying to catch some colourful butterfly or bird as it makes its winged way through the world, giving joy as it passes but never staying long enough to be caught and mounted.

A few random impressions from here and there may give a glimpse of her vitality.

Her visit to Pakistan was so heart-warming and inspiring. Its memories will always be cherished by every Scout and Guide. It seems that whoever came into contact with her during her tour of our country found in her a dynamic and charming personality. One of my friends who has nothing to do with Guides very aptly expressed herself when she said—"I know now why each one of you seem to be so inspired and so ready to live in the true spirit of the Movement."

From North Carolina, U.S.A.:

You have given me personally and the others much inspiration, courage and hope. Frankly I feel at this point as if I could just "set the world on fire" with Scouting. Needless to say your visit will be remembered for ever. Words are inadequate to express the effect of your personality, vivaciousness and realness of purpose upon me. I am sure that time will see even more wonderful results from your being here with us.

From Miami, U.S.A.:

This noble lady gave of her time, energy, charm, enthusiasm, faith and knowledge to us. She has ennobled all of us and we may possibly never be the same after her visit.

So much for the leaders, but what do the children themselves think of their Chief?

My fifteen year old daughter, to whom Guiding is all things, felt that you were "Interested in *me too*, Mother, although she is *of* the world. How does she give so much to each of us?"

A Scottish Patrol Leader, after a Rally:

She was not the kind of person I had imagined at all. She was not a fragile old lady but a gay jolly person full of humour. When she saw us first she waved gaily to us all. Then she told us how everybody she meets tells her that the Guide movement is excellent and they give her a pat on the back. She told us that it was *us* that made the Guide Movement and next minute she had everybody patting each other on the back. She told us how Guiding is a game but the best game in the world because it has a purpose.

Of this same visit a Scottish Commissioner gave her verdict:

It gave the Guides a tremendous thrill to see you and have you in their midst. Letters have streamed in from Guiders and Guides saying how lovely it was and what fun. Lots of them walked out on Sunday to say thank you to *me* for *you* which I thought rather sweet.
You'll be amused to hear that you had an unseen audience consisting of the drivers and guards of the four special trains, the Area Traffic Manager for British Railways, and about a dozen bus drivers,

all of whom sneaked in behind us. They were so impressed with the whole thing they just can't get over it. They couldn't quite understand how it was done, but "my worrd," they said, "you have something there"—and we have, haven't we!

A teacher in 1957 wrote:

I can never repay Guiding for what it has done for me. In some small measure I suppose I can, by handing on to my girls some of those vital qualities that I learned as a Girl Guide of about fourteen. It is fascinating to see that all the patrol challenges, the woodcraft, the wide games, the knotting, the hikes and the camp fires, mean as much to the present day Scout and Guide as they did to us. B-P's Scouting is more needed now than ever for the modern child is brought up with so many gadgets and press-button comforts that self-reliance and initiative are characteristics still often sadly lacking.

People sometimes admit to something that goes still deeper:

I had my first camp at Enniskerry, no place has ever given me such joy as did the Wicklow Hills . . . It was the outdoor side of Guiding which chiefly appealed to me, but it went deeper than that. Although during my twenty odd years of Guiding I had not really found Him, it mattered to me more than anything that the first clause of the Promise was "to do my duty to God". I am reminded of the verse "When in the slippery paths of youth with heedless steps I ran, Thine arm unseen upheld me still and led me up to man". Undoubtedly Guiding was one of the ways by which He led me. It is eleven years since I was active in the Movement but I do not have to look far to see its influence still with me.

"A scent of wood-smoke in the air, the old days coming back."
What magic that word "camp" spells to so many of the older generation today, especially to those who were "in it" when it was not all so easy. An elderly man said the other day: "I can still light a fire with one match. The book (*Scouting for Boys*) says two, but my Scoutmaster said that another match in hand would make us careless with the first one." His Scout camps were still green in his memory. For thousands of old Scouts and Guides, when much else is forgotten, the scent of

wood-smoke or the lilt of a song will always bring back a picture of laughing happy faces in the firelight and the memory of all the fun and friendship—*and* the hard work shared—of camp.

Wet or fine, hot or cold, be the weather what it will, camping will continue to be the high spot of any Guide Company or Scout Troop so long as the Movement exists.

What is there about this Girl Guide Movement—now past its Diamond Jubilee in the parent country and in some other countries too—which gives it so strong an appeal to girls of every sort and kind, of every creed and colour, and which gathers into its elastic net the children of parsonages and palaces, of homes and hospitals, of schools, reformatories, leper colonies and institutions for deaf, dumb or blind children—all flying the same flag and bound by the same Promise.

Surely it is that Scouting and Guiding are keys which open the door to the adventure sought by every lively child. That the adventure is legitimate and based on high ideals does not make it any less exciting, as is proved by the number of youngsters crowding in to join. Each year brings its rise in numbers and this would be even greater if there were more leaders to train them. But Guiding is breeding its own leaders now and those who have such happy memories as these letters describe are only too anxious that their children and grandchildren shall have the same opportunities.

A Singapore newspaper in 1969 said this:

In Guiding and its activities you discover things about yourself, about your surroundings and about your Creator. At the same time you develop your senses, your memory, your awareness of what goes on around you. This process of discovery and development continues throughout life and is part of all true education. Nothing is done by theory alone, everything depends on experience. Guiding awakens the personality of each individual.

So when people ask the Chief Guide why she carries on with her strenuous task she replies:

Because it seems to me to be my job still to do what I can, where I can, to help and encourage those who are giving so much to this wonderful game which my husband gave to us; and if, by my travels, I can still make their task a little easier, I shall go on travelling so long as God gives me the power to do it.

A tribute from an American Girl Scout was one which pleased Olave very much because one of her main objects has always been the forming of links in the great chain of friendship "of which I am privileged to hold one end".

Just as we feel that you leave a little bit of you everywhere that you visit, so we feel that you pass along a little bit of each place as you go. After your visit I personally felt closer to every place where you'd been. The world was a better and warmer place, more closely bound, because of Scouting and you. On mornings when there seems too much to do I shall remember you and your endless journeys bearing our torch.

To the Chief Guide the gatherings of Guides in large towns, where they have frequent opportunities of meeting, are of rather less importance than meetings in some of those places, overseas or in scattered rural districts, where her visit means the coming together for the first time of the little units, to make friends with one another and to realise that they are all comrades in the same game. "I am not only the Chief Guide," she will say, "but the Chief Excuse for such a get-together".

World friendship is, to her, one of the very important aspects of Guiding, and she loses no chance of preaching it.

"You are ambassadors, not only of Scouting and Guiding, but also of friendship, and it is your job, just as it is mine, to promote it."

So, cheered and uplifted by tributes from many lands, she goes on carrying out the task that her husband bequeathed to her. She did it first purely out of love for him, and when he was at hand to help and advise her. Now for thirty years she has done it alone, still for love of him but now also for love of this vast family of Scouts and Guides. Her devotion to everything connected with his ideas, or implicit in them, has never wavered, and in giving herself fully to the task she has found—as he prophesied she would—her life's happiness.

"I am the luckiest person in the world," she says, and no-one looking at her will want to deny it.

Perhaps her most outstanding quality is her faith in people, and her belief in inherent goodness. This is her secret, the thing that makes her

"tick", and her philosophy of life. It is a very simple belief, uncompli-
cated and sincere, and it is this that attracts so many people of all ages
to her.

B-P used to preach that the divine spark existed in every individual
soul, and that it was the business of the Scouter or Guider to search for
this and, having found it, to encourage and develop the spark until it
became a flame which nothing can extinguish. He would never believe
that any person created by God could be "written off" as a hopeless case.

Olave holds the same sort of belief. She has no inhibitions about
using the word "goodness" when she speaks of it not as something that
may be achieved in the distant future but as something which is already
present, only awaiting development, in every young person, because—
as she so often tells them—she spells "good" with one "o".

It is this belief of the Chief Guide's in their inherent worth that
stimulates so many people—grown-ups as well as children—to try to
live up to what she expects and believes of them. It is her faith in each
one of them, her finding of the best instead of fearing the worst, that
gives encouragement and hope to so many.

The American wife of the Military Attaché in Copenhagen wrote of
her:

> Just to think of her is to be encouraged and stimulated to be a
> better person for having thought of her. She is one of the great
> people of the world today, not just well-known but truly *great* in the
> highest sense of the word.

Yet Olave does not live in any fool's paradise. "See the worst but
look at the best" is her watchword—rather an unusual one today if one
were to judge only by newspapers and television programmes.

I think it is true to say that the majority of women depend, for at least
a part of their pleasure in life, on things which have not the slightest
appeal for this most unusual woman. She does not smoke, drink, play
bridge, or enjoy cocktail parties or race meetings.

As regards radio and television, it is for the most part a closed book
to her and she has certainly contributed far more to their programmes
than she has either watched or listened to. She has been interviewed by
most television "personalities" and given countless radio talks, for in
these media she finds a useful means of conveying her message.

April 1st 1963

I acted my small piece with Richard Dimbleby, that very nice good B.B.C. commentator. We did it in the sunk garden here. It took ages and we sat and talked and did the various bits literally from 11.45 till after 2 o'clock.

She enjoyed this meeting but that, as far as she was concerned, was the end of it.

Olave enjoys a good book or play but finds it rather difficult to appreciate modern drama or art forms.

Perhaps most "un-womanish" of all, she takes only the smallest interest in clothes, barely noticing what other people are wearing, and knows nothing at all of "war paint", "perms", or "window shopping".

The main duty of clothes, to her mind, is to last as long as possible and so to save the wearer the trouble and expense of replacing them.

Her mother used to complain that there was something strangely lacking in this daughter's make-up in her stubborn determination to "take no thought for raiment".

But uniform is to her quite another matter. She loves her uniform, more especially her "World Chief Guide" blue-grey, and feels far happier and more at ease when wearing this than when in mufti.

Uniform is to the World Chief Guide, as it was to the Founder, a very important part of the game and she loses no opportunity of impressing this on Scouts and Guides.

If you look at our Founder's plan as a whole you will get something of his vision of what the world would be like if everybody in it knew and kept to our Law and Promise and carried out those ideals and played the whole game properly. If you try to see the Movement as a whole, of which your own Company and neighbourhood is an important corner, you will understand better why certain things are expected of you, and why certain definite items have their part in the programme.

When an architect draws up his blueprint for a building he includes nothing that has not some important specific purpose, whether for beautifying the building, for adding strength to it, or for making it more valuable and useful.

In exactly the same way my husband—the Founder of the whole

plan—thought out this scheme with the utmost care, putting into it all that you need, and putting nothing into it that had not some quite definite reason underlying it. Each step in the training was carefully devised because—whether you realise it or not—it was going to teach you something and be of use to you, and, through you, to other people later on. All the many skills that you learn, and the badges that you earn, all the games that you play and the system of your work in patrols and Companies, are there not just by chance or because some-one thought they would be fun to do, but because each one has a special function in making up the training of a good Guide and a good citizen.

Now you might think that uniform is not of very great importance and that you can do your work and play your games and learn your crafts just as well in any old clothes. But that is not the point. Just as the salute, and the Promise, and the left hand-shake all have their special reason and significance, so too has the uniform.

First of course it was suggested as a practical dress for your activities.

Secondly, it encourages one to be smart, neat, and tidy. The polishing of badges and shoes, the washing and ironing of ties, help to a feeling of security and confidence in being correctly turned out. You can face the world with courage and your own personality is strengthened without your realising it.

Thirdly, uniform is a sign of service to the community. Those older people who hold responsible positions and do fine good things for others have a uniform as a sign of their calling—firemen, police-men, armed forces, nurses, Red Cross workers, and so on. And players in teams dress alike as an outward sign of the team spirit, for each one "plays in his place and plays the game" not for his own personal advantage or glorification but for his side.

And now, if you think again, you will realise that there is a fourth good reason for wearing uniform and taking pains over it, and taking pride in it too. Guides and Scouts, as you know, are of every sort and kind, of every creed and race and country and nation, and of every income group. The wearing of uniform covers up such distinctions and brings a feeling of "one-ness", so that when you meet in uniform

Driving from London Airport on her eightieth birthday

With her family at Westminster Abbey

Reading the lesson in
the Abbey, 1969

Surrounded by Guides as
she left the Abbey

it makes no difference whether you can afford expensive clothes or not, whether you come from a castle or a cottage—there is no possibility of anyone feeling out of it through not being so well dressed as others, and you find that you are friends immediately. There is unity as seen from outside as well as unity inside your minds and hearts.

Yes, to the Chief Guide, uniform has a definite value, and the eye that misses out on the mink coat and the decorative ear-rings, is quick to spot the well cared-for uniform, the neatly folded tie and the bright clean badge on a Guide or Brownie.

"I expect she will have lovely clothes," wistfully remarked an Australian Brownie when she heard that Princess Anne was to be enrolled by her aunt, the Princess Royal, and she was astonished and very thrilled to learn that, in Brownie uniform, the Princess would be dressed exactly like herself.

At a Girl Scout Rally in a place in America which shall be nameless, the Chief Guide, as inspecting officer, enquired whether a certain little group possessed no uniform as they were not wearing it. "Oh yes, they have it," was the answer, "but they keep it for special occasions!"

She is a stickler for uniform, and she also likes to see Guide badges or pins worn when out of uniform, partly because they are instant friend-ship-makers. A grown-up visitor to Hampton Court Palace will often be asked "Where is your badge?" if Olave happens to know that she was a Guide, because "Once a Guide always a Guide" and one should take pride in the fact. No detail of this kind misses her scrutiny and some of her fellow-residents in the royal apartments could tell tales of badges looked out and polished up for a lunch party, or of being enrolled with one of the Chief Guide's own badges if they have not been fortunate enough to "belong" in their youth.

Though she has this tremendous faith in young people and their potentialities, Olave does sometimes feel worried by the appearance of some of those who walk through the grounds of the Palace with unkempt hair, tatty inadequate clothing and sombre expressions. They are the ones that Scouting and Guiding have somehow failed to catch—perhaps through lack of leaders—and they make her feel guilty.

It has been suggested in earlier chapters that Olave Baden-Powell is a

N

great organiser—and this is very true. If one does not want to be organised into taking on some piece of work for which she feels one is fitted,
it is best to beware of her.

But it must be confessed that she is also, in her own words, something
of a disorganiser. Sometimes, at a Guide Rally or public meeting, she
will employ this gift rather to the apparent dismay of the promoters, if,
to her, the proceedings seem rather dull or too formal. If she feels that
the children will get stiff or bored from standing or sitting too long in
the same position, she will suggest movement—"Get up and shake
yourselves and run round, and then sit down again beside somebody
you don't know".

Or she may interpolate, in the middle of her impassioned address at
some public meeting—"Mr So-and-so you are not comfortable, come
and sit over here." She has been known to treat a whole row of Mayors
and Mayoresses rather like a set of chessmen, moving them from their
lordly seats on the platform and replacing them in pawn-like positions
in the front row where they can see and hear her better.

"I do a great deal of talking," she will say, "but I never make
speeches." It is quite true. She likes to wander along, without a written
script or even notes, unless it is a question of timing and space for the
B.B.C. or a translation into some other language. But there is always a
point in her talk, and something to get hold of.

Official Press and photographers, if they are too attentive, sometimes
get rather short shrift. "Now please *take* your picture, Mr Photographer,
and then go away. I can't talk when you are looking at me."

At a National Jamboree in America in 1969:

Mounting a redwood bench on the Avenue of Flags, she started giving
directions to one and all. "Kneel down now, you on the front row, and
take your picture and creep away; then the second row can get their
pictures. Don't get in each other's way, now. How many cameras are
there at the Jamboree?" "A million" was the answer. Then began
her auctioneer-like chant: "Nearly done, nearly done, nearly done?"
Finally they were done . . . Then, "two at a time" she shook hands
with all. With the left hand of one boy clasped atop the left hand of
the other. "Good luck, and have a happy time," she said to each.

Most people agree that when the Chief Guide takes a hand in

organising, disorganising and reorganising, it is all to the good. It cheers
up the proceedings, adds to the informality, makes everyone laugh, and
no-one bears any resentment. She is unique and cannot be expected to
behave in a stereotyped fashion!

After a visit to Athens for a World Conference, a Greek newspaper
summed up what all her Guide friends know about their World Chief in
these words:

> In 1930 the title of Chief Guide of the World was conferred upon
> Lady Baden-Powell . . . In her address to the members of the
> Conference she said "I will do my best to help everybody every-
> where".
>
> Ever since, this has been her one great aim in life. It is the impres-
> sion you get directly you face her energetic countenance. Generally
> great expectations are never fulfilled. In this case Lady Baden-
> Powell's personality proved irresistible: a smile full of kindness and
> faith, two bright eager eyes, hands that instinctively "give the hand",
> a tireless vitality that is always ready, an indomitable wish to serve . . .
> Thus she was seen, greeted and loved by the Greek Girl Guides of
> Athens, Epiros, Macedonia.

The author has tried in these pages to give something of a picture of a
very unusual but lovable personality. If she has been made to appear
austere, one-track-minded, or out of touch with modern life, this has
been far from the intention. She is none of those things, but she just
has not the ability, the desire, or the time to be exactly like other people.
She is a leader and not a follower, except of that one person, her
husband. But though an exception herself to so many rules and
conventions she grudges nothing to her friends that gives them
enjoyment, even if she cannot quite understand where the enjoyment
lies.

Her eightieth birthday in 1969 marked also her fiftieth year of World
Guide leadership. In all these fifty years and more she has never spared
herself, never put personal pursuits or pleasures before her task but has
brought in her every gift, material, moral, and spiritual, to help in its
promotion. And in doing this she has built up a very large army of
friends and supporters.

And when she leaves her Palace "perch" and flies away to see her beloved family far afield, there is a dismal blank in the apartment, and her staff and friends begin to count the weeks and days that must elapse before a plane will deposit her once more at London Airport.

For all the world loves a charmer.

FLIGHTS BY THE WORLD CHIEF TO VISIT GUIDES

		Miles
1931	1. New Zealand. Lake Taupo to Rotorua	38
1932	2. Breslau, Germany, via Berlin to England	910
1935	3. Nyeri, Kenya, to Dar-es-Salaam	600
1936	4. Cape Town to Durban	565
1938	5. Nairobi to Lusaka, N. Rhodesia	179
	6. Lusaka to Mankoya	240
	7. Mankoya to Lusaka	240
	8. Lusaka to Salisbury, S. Rhodesia	244
	9. Salisbury to Broken Hill and	
	10. Broken Hill to Nairobi	1,422
	11. London to Berne, Switzerland	499
	12. Berne to London	499
1942	13. Mombasa, Kenya, to Durban	1,050
1943	14. Liverpool to Isle of Man	108
	15. Isle of Man to Liverpool	108
	16. Thurso to Orkneys	30
	17. Orkneys to Aberdeen	129
1944	18. London to Dublin	263
	19. Dublin to London	263
1945	20. Marseilles to Rome	397
	21. Rome to Florence	198
	22. Florence to Rome	198
	23. Rome to Paris via Marseilles	754
	24. Brussels to London	213
	25. London to Zurich, Switzerland	516
	26. Zurich to London, but owing to fog could not land so back to Paris	731
	27. Paris to London	215

1946	28. New York to Miami, Florida	1,227
	29. Bahamas to Miami	130
	30. Miami to Cuba	235
	31. Cuba to Miami	235
	32. Miami to Mexico City	1,345
	33. Mexico City to Miami	1,345
	34. Miami to Jamaica	539
	35. Jamaica via Venezuela to Trinidad	1,400
	36. Trinidad to Barbados	214
	37. Barbados to Trinidad	214
	38. Tobago to Port of Spain, Trinidad	53
	39. Trinidad to Georgetown, British Guiana	383
	40. *Wasp* to New Amsterdam and back	90
	41. *Wasp* to Cabacaburi, Mackenzie, etc.	150
	42. Georgetown to Trinidad	383
	43. Trinidad to Miami	1,836
	44. Miami via Washington to Philadelphia	1,900
	45. Cincinnati to Washington	587
	46. Toronto across Canada to Vancouver	2,237
	47. Monkton to Prince Edward Island	833
	48. Charlottetown to Summerside	80
	49. Charlottetown back to mainland	80
	50. Gander, Newfoundland to England	2,344
	51. Zurich, Switzerland to Prague	556
	52. Prague to Amsterdam	881
	53. Amsterdam to England	229
	54. London to Dublin	263
	55. Dublin to Liverpool	139
1947	56. Perth, W. Australia to Geraldton	230
	57. Geraldton to Perth	230
	58. Port Pirrie to Whyalla	30
	59. Whyalla to Port Pirrie	30
	60. Perth to Adelaide	1,415
	61. Adelaide to Port Gambier	220
	62. Melbourne to Sydney, N.S.W.	478
	63. Sydney to Wagga Wagga	227

	100. Athens to Cyprus	400
	101. Cyprus to Cairo	450
	102. Alexandria to Khartoum	1,500
	103. Khartoum to Kenya	1,062
1950	104. Entebbe to Nairobi	280
	105. Nairobi to Arusha	144
	106. Arusha to Dar-es-Salaam	457
	107. Dar-es-Salaam to Zanzibar	47
	108. Zanzibar to Mombasa	184
	109. Mombasa to Nairobi	251
	110. Nairobi to Ndola	1,011
	111. Lusaka to Mzimba	455
	112. Mzimba to Zomba	260
	113. Blantyre to Salisbury	300
	114. Salisbury to Umtali	130
	115. Umtali to Fort Victoria	150
	116. Fort Victoria to Gwelo	81
	117. Gwelo to Bulawayo	85
	118. Bulawayo to Johannesburg	430
	119. Johannesburg to Carolina	160
	120. Carolina to Johannesburg	160
	121. Johannesburg to Kimberley	269
	122. Durban to East London	290
	123. East London to Port Elizabeth	150
	124. Port Elizabeth to George	423
	125. George to Cape Town	200
	126. Cape Town to Salisbury	1,464
	127. Salisbury to Ndola	412
	128. Ndola to Elizabethville	120
	129. Elizabethville to Leopoldville	1,065
	130. Brazzaville to Douala	1,206
	131. Douala to Lagos	485
	132. In Nigeria	—
	133. Lagos to Calabar	386
	134. Calabar to Lagos	386
	135. Lagos to Kaduna	787
	136. Kaduna to Jos and Port Harcourt and back to Lagos	492

	173. Lexington to Columbos, Ohio	150
	174. Pittsburgh to New York	225
	175. Philadelphia to Dallas (Texas)	1,300
	176. Wichita to Topeka	180
	177. London to Berne	520
1953	178. Berne via Copenhagen to Oslo	1,000
	179. Oslo to England	750
	180. London to Bourget, France	215
	181. Le Touquet to London	110
	182. Halifax, Nova Scotia to Sydney	265
	183. New Glasgow to Charlottetown	59
	184. Charlottetown to Monckton	122
	185. St John, New Brunswick to Halifax	297
	186. Halifax to St John's (Newfoundland)	550
	187. St John's to Boston, Mass.	897
	188. Corning to Philadelphia	187
	189. Milwaukee to Caspar, Wyoming	1,197
	190. Caspar to Waterloo, Iowa	801
	191. Waterloo to Chicago, Ill.	396
	192. Chicago to Rochester	598
	193. Savannah, Georgia to Miami	600
	194. Miami to Pensacola	615
	195. Houston, Texas to Midland	516
	196. Midland to Alburquerque	400
	197. El Peso to Wichita	795
	198. Memphis to New Orleans	425
	199. Tampa to Miami	269
	200. Miami to Bahamas	200
	201. Bahamas to Miami	200
	202. Miami to New York	1,346
	203. Wichita to Boston, Mass.	1,665
1954	204. London to Nice	647
	205. Nice to London	647
	206. London to Malmo, Sweden	623
	207. Malmo to Zurich	621
	208. Geneva to Amsterdam	393

209. Amsterdam to London   230
210. London to Belfast   334
211. Belfast to Isle of Man   73
212. Isle of Man to Belfast   73
213. Belfast to London   334
214. Basle to London   436
215. London to Stockholm   900
216. Stockholm to London   900
217. London to Montreal   3,371

1955 218. Winnipeg to Flin-Flon   500
      219. Flin-Flon to Winnipeg   500

1956 220. El Paso (Texas) to Chilhuahua, Mexico ⎤
      221. Chilhuahua to Torreon   ⎟
      222. Torreon to Mexico City   ⎬ 2,600
      223. Mexico City to Monterrey   ⎟
      224. Monterrey to Laredo   ⎦
      225. London to Geneva   470
      226. Geneva to London   470
      227. London to Reykjavik   1,110
      228. Reykjavik to London   1,100
      229. London to Frankfurt   400
      230. Hamburg to London   406
      231. London to Malta   1,372
      232. Malta to Tripoli   222
      233. Tripoli to Rome   650
      234. Rome to Khartoum   2,165
      235. Khartoum to Entebbe   1,090
      236. Entebbe to Gulu   200
      237. Gulu to Entebbe   200
      238. Entebbe to Nairobi   320
      239. Nairobi to Nyeri   360
      240. Nairobi to Abercorn   664
      241. Lusaka to Fort Jameson   47
      242. Lilongwe to Blantyre   218
      243. Lilongwe to Karonga   297
      244. Karonga to Lilongwe   297

281.	Sydney to Williamstown	100
282.	Williamstown to Sydney	100
283.	Sydney to Parkes	190
284.	Parkes to Dubbo	60
285.	Dubbo to Sydney	260
286.	Sydney to Casino	331
287.	Brisbane to Cairns	1,230
288.	Cairns to Rockhampton	150
289.	Townsville to Brisbane	980
290.	Brisbane to Port Moresby (Papua)	1,300
291.	Port Moresby to Lae	200
292.	Lae to Lorengau	400
293.	Lorengau to Rabaul	340
294.	Rabaul to Lae	420
295.	Lae to Port Moresby	190
296.	Port Moresby to Sydney	1,700
297.	Sydney to Canberra	245
298.	Canberra to Sydney	245
299.	Sydney to Nandi (Fiji)	1,985
300.	Nandi to Suva	100
301.	Suva to Nandi	100
302.	Nandi to Sydney	1,985
303.	Sydney to Manila, Philippines	4,166
304.	Manila to Hong-Kong	715
305.	Hong-Kong to Singapore	2,000
306.	Singapore to Kuala Lumpur	197
307.	Kuala Lumpur to Khota Bahru	339
308.	Khota Bahru to Penang	152
309.	Penang to Kuala Lumpur	187
310.	Kuala Lumpur to Malacca	75
311.	Malacca to Singapore	126
312.	Singapore to Labaun (Sarawak)	879
313.	Labaun to Tawau	200
314.	Tawau to Sandakan	100
315.	Sandakan to Jesselton (North Borneo)	200
316.	Jesselton to Kuching	389
317.	Kuching to Singapore	449

	318. Singapore to Colombo	1,757
	319. Colombo to Jaffna and back	350
	320. Colombo to London—via Bombay	5,880
	321. London to Berne via Zurich	556
	322. Berne via Zurich to Brussels	362
	323. Brussels to London	213
1959	324. London to Kenya via Khartoum, Entebbe	4,000
	325. Kenya to London	4,000
	326. Edinburgh to London	350
	327. London to Manchester	160
	328. Manchester to Belfast	150
	329. Belfast to London	310
	330. London to Recife, Brazil	6,400
	331. Recife to Salvador, Bahia	410
	332. Salvador to Rio de Janeiro	1,022
	333. Rio to Sao Paulo	231
	334. Sao Paulo to Porte Alegre	523
	335. Porte Alegre to Monte Video	300
	336. Montevideo to Buenos Aires	140
	337. Buenos Aires to Santiago	680
	338. Santiago to Lima, Peru	1,600
	339. Lima to Guayaquil, Ecuador	700
	340. Guayaquil to Bogota	900
	341. Bogota to Medellin	250
	342. Medellin to Panama	300
	343. Panama to San Jose	280
	344. San Jose to Managua	218
	345. Managua to Guatemala	339
	346. Guatemala to Belize	350
	347. Belize to San Salvador	450
	348. San Salvador to Mexico City	775
	349. Mexico City to Los Angeles	1,582
	350. New York to London	3,500
	(21,050 miles on this 1959 trip)	
	351. London to Dublin	300
	352. Dublin to London	300

1960	353. London to Gibraltar	1,150
	354. Gibraltar via Tangiers to Lisbon	550
	355. Lisbon to London	750
	356. London to Munich	652
	357. Munich to London	603
	358. London to Guernsey	300
	359. Guernsey to Jersey and	
	360. Jersey to London	400
	361. London to Athens	1,010
	362. Athens to Zurich	1,110
	363. Zurich to Helsinki via Copenhagen	800
	364. Helsinki to London	1,100
	365. London to Copenhagen	600
	366. 7 hops in a helicopter	200
	367. Copenhagen to London	600
	368. London to Lagos	2,765
	369. Lagos to Enugu	400
	370. Enugu to Lagos via Port Harcourt	700
	371. Lagos to Kano and on	
	372. thence to London	2,765
	373. London to Wildenrath	320
	374. Return by R.A.F.	320
	375. London to Beirut	2,432
	376. Beirut to Karachi	2,162
	377. Karachi to Lahore	830
	378. Lahore to Peshawar	275
	379. Peshawar to Rawalpindi	110
	380. Rawalpindi to Lahore	165
	381. Delhi to Bangalore	1,110
	382. Bangalore to Coimbatore	100
	383. Coimbatore to Cochin	120
	384. Cochin to Madras	406
1961	385. Madras to Calcutta	760
	386. Calcutta to Dacca	144
	387. Dacca to Chittagong	160
	388. Chittagong to Rangoon	472

389.	Rangoon to Mandalay	400
390.	Mandalay to Rangoon	400
391.	Rangoon to Bassein	140
392.	Bassein to Rangoon	140
393.	Rangoon to Delhi	1,750
394.	Delhi to Agra	130
395.	Agra to Delhi	130
396.	Delhi to Jaipur	160
397.	Jaipur to Delhi	160
398.	Delhi to Lucknow	305
399.	Agra to Calcutta	740
400.	Calcutta to Bombay	1,540
401.	Bombay to Hyderabad	640
402.	Hyderabad to Colombo	780
403.	Colombo to Galoya	180
404.	Galoya to Colombo	180
405.	Colombo to Bombay	1,111
406.	Bombay to Rome	3,830
407.	Rome to Milan and	
408.	on to London	1,000
409.	London to New York	3,500
410.	Philadelphia to Buffalo	300
411.	Buffalo to Rochester	80
412.	Rochester to Boston	430
413.	Boston to Montreal	270
414.	Montreal to St John's	1,050
415.	Newfoundland to Halifax	220
416.	Halifax to Monckton	192
417.	New Brunswick to Gander	320
418.	Gander to St John's and	180
419.	Charlottetown, Prince Edward Island	140
420.	Toronto to Winnipeg	948
421.	Winnipeg to Regina	350
422.	Regina to Edmonton	377
423.	Edmonton to Vancouver	650
424.	Vancouver to Calgary	900
425.	Calgary to Toronto	1,775

	462.	Ndola to Livingstone	400
	463.	Livingstone to Mongu	230
	464.	Mongu to Lusaka	300
	465.	Lusaka to Salisbury	221
	466.	Salisbury to Blantyre	300
	467.	Blantyre to Dar-es-Salaam	705
	468.	Dar-es-Salaam to Nairobi	470
	469.	Nairobi to Entebbe	325
	470.	Entebbe to London	4,036
	471.	London to Copenhagen	649
	472.	Copenhagen to London	649
	473.	London to Athens	1,010
	474.	Athens to Rhodes	500
	475.	Rhodes to Athens	500
	476.	Athens to London	1,010
	477.	London to Isle of Man	253
	478.	Isle of Man to Ulster	65
	479.	Ulster to London	400
	480.	London to Bermuda	3,096
	481.	Bermuda to Nassau, Bahamas	920
	482.	Nassau to Miami	185
1964	483.	San Antonio to Mexico	900
	484.	Mexico City to Tampico	490
	485.	Tampico to Mexico	490
	486.	Mexico to Miami	1,500
	487.	Miami to Montego Bay	465
	488.	Jamaica to Curacao	160
	489.	Curacao to Caracas	160
	490.	Caracas to Puerto Ordaz	350
	491.	Puerto Ordaz to Caracas	350
	492.	Caracas to Curacao	160
	493.	Curacao to Surinam	960
	494.	Surinam to Cayenne	300
	495.	Cayenne to Georgetown	420
	496.	Georgetown to New Amsterdam	80
	497.	New Amsterdam to Georgetown	80

498. Georgetown to Mackenzie   120
499. Mackenzie to Georgetown   120
500. Georgetown to Trinidad   310
501. Trinidad to Barbados   220
502. Barbados to St Lucia   110
503. St Lucia to Domenica   90
504. Domenica to Antigua   105
505. Antigua to St Kitts   70
506. St Kitts to Anguilla   50
507. Anguilla to Montserrat   60
508. Montserrat to Antigua   50
509. Antigua to St Vincent   100
510. St Vincent to Grenada   150
511. Grenada to Trinidad   110
512. Trinidad to Tobago   50
513. Tobago to Trinidad   50
514. Port of Spain to Port Fortin   60
515. Trinidad to New York   2,310
516. New York to London   3,456
517. London to Berlin   655
518. Berlin to London   655
519. London to New York   3,456

1965 520. New York to London   3,456
521. London to Rome   885
522. Rome to Tel Aviv   1,400
523. Tel Aviv to Ankara   700
524. Ankara to Tel Aviv   700
525. Tel Aviv to Nairobi   4,050
526. Nairobi to Mauritius   1,925
527. Mauritius to Nairobi   1,925
528. Nairobi to Voi   200
529. Voi to Nairobi   200
530. Nairobi to Entebbe   323
531. Entebbe to Khartoum   640
532. Khartoum to Cairo   1,400
533. Cairo to London   1,100

534.	Penzance to the Scillies	40
535.	Scillies to Penzance	40
536.	London to Luxembourg	200
537.	Luxembourg to Oslo	300
538.	Oslo to Stockholm	540
539.	Stockholm to Oslo	540
540.	Oslo to Trondhjem	350
541.	Trondhjem to Oslo	350
542.	Oslo to London	760
543.	Penzance to Scillies	40
544.	Scillies to Penzance	40
545.	London to Toronto	3,000
546.	San Diego to San Antonio	1,285
547.	San Antonio to Mexico	700
548.	Mexico to Panama	1,600
549.	Panama to El Salvador	563
550.	El Salvador to British Honduras	350
551.	Belize to Guatemala	350
552.	Guatemala to Mexico	708
553.	Mexico to Houston, Texas	666
554.	Knoxville to Spartenberg	350
555.	Spartenberg to Lexington	250
556.	Louisville to St Louis	270
557.	St Louis to Oklahoma	460
558.	Wichita to Little Rock	550
559.	Little Rock to Washington	1,000
560.	Washington to Newark	150
561.	New York to Boston	225
562.	Boston to London	3,000

1966
563.	London to Amsterdam	150
564.	Amsterdam to London	150
565.	London to Zurich	565
566.	Basle to London	436
567.	London to Tokyo	8,481
568.	Tokyo to Seoul	1,000
569.	Seoul to Tokyo	1,000

570. Tokyo to Hong-Kong — 2,872
571. Hong-Kong to Manila — 701
572. Manila to Bangkok — 1,400
573. Bangkok to Bombay — 1,790
574. Bombay to Goa — 275
575. Goa to Bombay — 275
576. Bombay to Ahmedabad — 240
577. Ahmedabad to Delhi — 384
578. Delhi to London — 5,750

1967
579. London to Mexico — 5,849
580. Mexico to New Zealand — 8,247
581. Auckland to Wellington — 325
582. Wellington to Christchurch — 200
583. Christchurch to Wellington — 200
584. Wellington to Auckland — 325
585. Auckland to Palmerston North — 250
586. Wellington to Melbourne — 1,560
587. Melbourne to Canberra — 295
588. Canberra to Melbourne — 295
589. Melbourne to Hobart — 490
590. Launceston to Melbourne — 375
591. Melbourne to Sydney — 450
592. Sydney to Brisbane — 473
593. Brisbane to Darwin — 1,832
594. Darwin to Adelaide — 2,000
595. Adelaide to Perth — 1,340
596. Perth to London — 11,563

1968
597. London to New York — 3,450
598. New York to Montreal — 600
599. Montreal to Chicago — 762
600. Chicago to Spokane — 1,511
601. Spokane to Seattle — 300
602. Seattle to Toronto — 3,320
603. Toronto to London — 3,000
604. London to Malta — 1,470
605. Malta to Rome — 580

	606. Rome to Entebbe	3,143
	607. Entebbe to Kisumu via Jinja	110
	608. Nairobi to Bombay	2,860
	609. Bombay to Colombo	970
	610. Colombo to Bombay	970
	611. Bombay to London	4,900
	612. London to Geneva	489
	613. Basle to London	436
	614. London to Nairobi	4,328
1969	615. Nairobi to Kisumu	200
	616. Kisumu to Nairobi	200
	617. Nairobi to London	4,328
	618. London to Helsinki	1,157
	619. Helsinki to London	1,157
	620. London to New York	3,450
	621. New York to Spokane	2,220
	622. Spokane to Vancouver	350
	623. Vancouver to Saskatoon	740
	624. Saskatoon to Toronto	1,374
	625. Toronto to Doe Lake	150
	626. Doe Lake to Toronto	150
	627. Toronto to London	3,557
	628. London to Helsinki	1,157
	629. Helsinki to London	1,157
	630. London to Lagos	2,765
	631. Lagos to London	2,765
	632. London to Brussels	213
	633. Brussels to London	213
	634. London to Guernsey,	
	635. Jersey and back	400
1970	636. London to Nairobi	4,628
	637. Nairobi to Dar-es-Salaam	500
	638. Dar-es-Salaam to Nairobi	500
	639. Nairobi to Johannesburg	1,861
	640. Johannesburg to Cape Town	790

641. Cape Town to Port Elizabeth   401
642. Port Elizabeth to East London   143
643. East London to Kimberley   345
644. Welhousen to Johannesburg   100
645. Johannesburg to Windhoek   724
646. Windhoek to Johannesburg   724
647. Johannesburg to Durban   313
648. Johannesburg to London   6,489

CHILDREN, GRANDCHILDREN and GREAT-GRANDCHILDREN
of OLAVE LADY BADEN-POWELL, WORLD CHIEF GUIDE

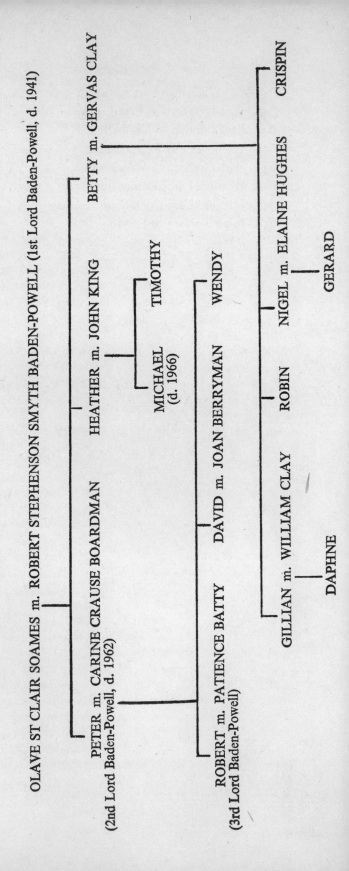

OLAVE ST CLAIR SOAMES m. ROBERT STEPHENSON SMYTH BADEN-POWELL (1st Lord Baden-Powell, d. 1941)

PETER m. CARINE CRAUSE BOARDMAN
(2nd Lord Baden-Powell, d. 1962)

HEATHER m. JOHN KING

BETTY m. GERVAS CLAY

MICHAEL
(d. 1966)

TIMOTHY

ROBERT m. PATIENCE BATTY
(3rd Lord Baden-Powell)

DAVID m. JOAN BERRYMAN

WENDY

GILLIAN m. WILLIAM CLAY

ROBIN

NIGEL m. ELAINE HUGHES

CRISPIN

DAPHNE

GERARD

Index